HBR Guide to
Better Mental Health at Work

Harvard Business Review Guides

Arm yourself with the advice you need to succeed on the job, from the most trusted brand in business. Packed with how-to essentials from leading experts, the HBR Guides provide smart answers to your most pressing work challenges.

The titles include:

HBR Guide for Women at Work

HBR Guide to Being a Great Boss

HBR Guide to Being More Productive

HBR Guide to Better Business Writing

HBR Guide to Better Mental Health at Work

HBR Guide to Building Your Business Case

HBR Guide to Buying a Small Business

HBR Guide to Changing Your Career

HBR Guide to Coaching Employees

HBR Guide to Collaborative Teams

HBR Guide to Data Analytics Basics for Managers

HBR Guide to Dealing with Conflict

HBR Guide to Delivering Effective Feedback

HBR Guide to Emotional Intelligence

HBR Guide to Finance Basics for Managers

HBR Guide to Getting the Mentoring You Need

HBR Guide to Getting the Right Job

HBR Guide to Getting the Right Work Done

HBR Guide to Leading Teams

HBR Guide to
Better Mental Health at Work

HARVARD BUSINESS REVIEW PRESS

Boston, Massachusetts

Copyright 2022 Harvard Business School Publishing Corporation

All rights reserved

Printed in the United States of America

1 2022

No part of this publication may be reproduced, stored in or introduced into a retrieval system, or transmitted, in any form, or by any means (electronic, mechanical, photocopying, recording, or otherwise), without the prior permission of the publisher. Requests for permission should be directed to permissions@harvardbusiness.org, or mailed to Permissions, Harvard Business School Publishing, 60 Harvard Way, Boston, Massachusetts 02163.

The web addresses referenced in this book were live and correct at the time of the book's publication but may be subject to change.

Library of Congress Cataloging-in-Publication Data

Names: Harvard Business Review Press, issuing body.
Title: HBR guide to better mental health at work / Harvard Business Review.
Other titles: Harvard Business Review guide to better mental health at work | Harvard business review guides.
Description: Boston, Massachusetts : Harvard Business Review Press, [2022] | Series: HBR guides | Includes index. |
Identifiers: LCCN 2022010822 (print) | LCCN 2022010823 (ebook) | ISBN 9781647823269 (paperback) | ISBN 9781647823276 (epub)
Subjects: LCSH: Quality of work life—Psychological aspects. | Employees—Mental health. | Psychology, Pathological. | Stigma (Social psychology) | Work—Psychological aspects. | Personnel management.
Classification: LCC HF5548.8 .H364 2022 (print) | LCC HF5548.8 (ebook) | DDC 158.7—dc23/eng/20220610
LC record available at https://lccn.loc.gov/2022010822
LC ebook record available at https://lccn.loc.gov/2022010823

ISBN: 978-1-64782-326-9

eISBN: 978-1-64782-327-6

The paper used in this publication meets the requirements of the American National Standard for Permanence of Paper for Publications and Documents in Libraries and Archives Z39.48-1992.

What You'll Learn

Not long ago, mental health challenges were something many of us felt we had to hide at work. If we were struggling, or a colleague was, the common reaction was to downplay or politely ignore it. But more and more companies are recognizing the importance of supporting employees' mental health and treating it as exactly what it is—an essential part of health.

This welcome shift is making it a little easier for us to be our authentic selves at work. But supporting mental health—for you, your teammates, and your employees—isn't always easy. How do you take care of your mental health while getting your job done? Start honest, productive conversations about mental health without overstepping? Cultivate a culture where stigma has no place? Help colleagues when you don't know how to help? And what about making sure company policies offer *all* employees what they need?

Whether you're an individual contributor, a manager, or a senior leader, this guide will help you create a workplace where people can be honest about how they're really doing. You'll learn how to:

- Talk openly about mental health at work

- Manage employees with different mental health challenges

- Approach a colleague who may be struggling

- Structure your days to support your mental health

- Build community with an employee resource group

- Understand how intersectionality affects mental health

- Respond to a panic attack at the office

- Ensure your company offers the benefits employees need

- Write a mental health policy that gives people tangible support

- Be an ally to your coworkers

Contents

Contents

SECTION FOUR

Supporting Mental Health as a Manager

Contents

Our Mental Health at Work

by Morra Aarons-Mele

For all the enthusiastic leadership posts that demand we "bring our whole self to work," most of us leave a big and important piece of ourselves at home every day: our mental health. Despite many positive developments around physical wellness in both leadership models (like fostering psychological safety and being a servant leader) and amenities (like standing desks and flexible hours), there is still a stigma associated with talking openly about mental health. There's endless literature on how to be more productive, defuse conflict, and get paid what you're worth, and precious little insight on how we humans can be fully human in one of the places we spend a great deal of time: work.

In the course of our lives, most of us will probably be both mentally well and mentally ill. You may be anxious

or depressed for a short time or because of circumstances, or you may have a diagnosed disorder that stays
with you for the duration. Each year in the United States,
anxiety disorders affect some 40 million adults, and
across the globe the number is an estimated 284 million people, making anxiety the most common mental
health ailment in the world. In reality the numbers are
surely far higher, as these statistics reflect only the people who were able to access treatment and who received
a diagnosis. Other mental health conditions include depression, mood disorders like bipolar I and II, obsessive
compulsive disorder, and conditions like post-traumatic
stress disorder (PTSD).

Some mental illnesses even travel together. Data from
the World Health Organization (WHO) indicates that
anxiety and depression—leading causes of disability
throughout the world—are closely linked, with 61.2% of
people who experienced an anxiety disorder in their life-
times also experiencing a major depressive disorder.

Of course, many of these conditions have become
more common in recent years because of the Covid-19
pandemic. On the whole, we are more anxious than
ever. Rates of anxiety, psychological distress, depression, insomnia, and PTSD all climbed throughout the
crisis; a study from Mental Health America found that
from 2019 to 2020, the number of people seeking help
for anxiety and depression increased 93%. Even more
recently, researchers found that global rates of anxiety
and depression climbed dramatically in 2020 due to the
pandemic, with an additional 76.2 million anxiety disorders and 53.2 million additional cases of major depressive disorder.

What is evident is that anxiety, depression, and other mental health issues can drain our energy, wreck our concentration, and drive us to make poor, rushed, and ill-considered judgments. They can lead us to focus on the wrong things, distort the facts, and jump to conclusions, and can even result in physical pain and injury. In more extreme situations, they can trap us in obsessive, negative thought loops that keep us from moving forward. They can lead us to dwell so much on frightening worst-case outcomes that we—and thus those we lead—become frozen. In short, unmanaged mental illness can make leaders and teams less effective. Not to mention it makes us deeply unhappy, at work and anywhere else.

Mental illness is a challenge, but it is not a weakness. When you understand your mental health and take it seriously, you will build strength for the long haul, ensuring your professional life is a more holistic part of your personal beliefs and goals. Many of us who have long histories with mental health challenges come to see them as a sort of superpower, obstacles that have helped us build resiliency and empathy and become the leaders we are proud to be. I credit my anxiety and bipolar disorder with great empathy, attunement, and interpersonal skills, tools that have helped me build a successful career as a marketer, salesperson, entrepreneur, and podcast host. Understanding your psyche is key to your leadership and success.

If there is one silver lining in the traumatic effects of the Covid-19 pandemic, it's that we can no longer pretend everything is fine. This means leaders have a generational opportunity to prioritize mental health at work and to start talking about what it looks like and how it manifests in our everyday professional lives.

Making Mental Health a Normal Part of Work

If you're reading this book, you're ready to do your part in a collective effort to make mental health discussions a normal part of day-to-day work. You know that this is difficult and summons powerful emotions. Indeed, many of the chapters in this book include personal sharing or disclosure by the author, because the best way to reduce stigma is to talk about our own experiences.

There's urgency to doing so: Given the numbers, it's safe to assume you currently work with multiple people who are in the midst of experiencing a mental health issue. They're our colleagues, direct reports, competitors, assistants, bosses, board members. They're us. They're the people running every business. And you yourself might be among them.

Reading this book will give you the tools and language you need to create the space for productive conversations around mental health.

A London School of Economics study found employees who can talk with their managers about their mental illness are more productive.[1] A lack of open conversation was associated with employees taking an additional 4.1 days off during an episode of depression. WHO estimates that, together, depression and anxiety cost the global economy $1 trillion per year in lost productivity—and that estimate is based on prepandemic data.

The good news is that more companies are getting it: Talking about mental health at work is healthy, and creating mentally healthy organizations is hard but possible. In a recent survey by Mind Share Partners, 65% of employees said they talked about their mental health in 2021. Companies are also investing more in mental health treatments. In this book, you will hear from leaders who are implementing mental health work practices.

You don't have to be perfect to be a great leader or great at your job. But you do have to be honest about who you are and what you need. We can all work together to understand mental health and take it seriously. Welcome to the conversation! Change starts with us.

How to Use This Book

You don't need to read this book cover to cover (but of course we'd love it if you did). Feel free to read the chapters that seem most relevant, or dip in and out as you want. If there's a specific section that really speaks to you and your organization, you can share it with decision makers, and maybe you'll even help form an employee resource group (ERG); there's more about ERGs in chapter 20. Or, you could start a book club with this guide and use it as a catalyst for discussions in your team or organization.

While every section of the book doesn't have advice for specific social identities in the workforce, we have tried to write this guide with diversity, inclusion, and belonging in mind. The mental health field as a whole has much work to do when it comes to treating people with

If you're looking for more resources, you might want to check out:

- National Alliance on Mental Illness—https://www.nami.org/home

- American Psychological Association—https://www.apa.org

- Anxiety.org—https://www.anxiety.org

- Anxiety and Depression Association of America—https://adaa.org

- Mind Share Partners—https://www.mindsharepartners.org

- Made of Millions—https://www.madeofmillions.com

- PRADAA Lab—https://sites.google.com/view/pradaalab/home

- ADDitude Mag—https://www.additudemag.com

- Understood—https://www.understood.org

- Mental Health America—https://www.mhanational.org

- Writer and former clinical psychologist Alice Boyes—http://www.aliceboyes.com

You might also check out the archive of *The Anxious Achiever*, the podcast on mental health that I host for the HBR Presents podcast network. I interview business leaders who struggle with all kinds of mental health challenges and disabilities. You can find the show at https://hbr.org or wherever you listen to podcasts.

an intersectional approach, and workplace mental health is no exception. The book's contents are focused on evidence-based advice, while narrowing in on specific groups when needed; the good news is that data shows this advice is usually broadly applicable.

I want to close with the wise words of one of my favorite podcast guests, Vikas Shah, OBE. Vikas is the ultimate high achiever, an entrepreneur, public figure, and MBA professor who has been honored by Queen Elizabeth for contributions to business and the economy in the U.K. He also manages anxiety and depression every single day. He is committed to sharing his experience in the hopes that it helps others manage better.

> *I was so anxious about work, about everything, and there was so much stress. And the burnout from anxiety depleted my emotional reserves so much that I ended up depressed as well. I'm really grateful that I was able to make peace with it, because that's not a narrative that we're told enough when we're talking about mental health. There's always this sense of recovery being an endpoint, whereas recovery in many cases is just making peace with whatever it is that caused you to be in that situation, and you have to learn to live with it and manage it. Making peace with the fact of who I am gives me superpowers, which I'm very grateful for. I have medication and I have my routine; I have the various things I do just to protect my mental health. It works. And it keeps me functioning relatively normally. Now I teach at business schools and I always say to the students, "If there's one thing I urge you to do,*

it is build resilience. It's the most important life skill you will ever have."

—Vikas Shah, OBE, on *The Anxious Achiever,*
season 4, episode 6

———————

Morra Aarons-Mele is an entrepreneur, online marketing expert, and communications executive who founded the award-winning strategic communications agency Women Online and The Mission List, an influencer database. She helped Hillary Clinton log on for her first internet chat, and has launched digital campaigns for former President Obama, Malala Yousafzai, the United Nations, and many other leading figures and organizations. An extremely anxious introvert herself, Morra hosts the top-rated podcast *The Anxious Achiever* for HBR Presents from *Harvard Business Review.* She's passionate about helping people rethink the relationship between their mental health and their leadership.

NOTE

1. Haroon Siddique, "Depressed Workers More Productive If They Can Talk to Their Bosses," *Guardian,* July 23, 2018, https://www.theguardian.com/society/2018/jul/23/depressed-workers-more-productive-if-they-can-talk-to-their-bosses.

Having Conversations About Mental Health

CHAPTER 1

Talking About Your Mental Health at Work

by Kelly Greenwood

By the time I disclosed my generalized anxiety disorder at work, it was too late. It had spiraled into debilitating depression, and I could no longer even craft a basic email, much less do the rigorous job I was hired for. My previously high performance had very noticeably suffered, compelling me to nervously share the truth and ultimately forcing me out on a leave of absence.

In retrospect, an accommodation early on likely could've prevented all of that, saving me tremendous personal turmoil and my organization the extra workload.

Adapted from "How to Talk About Your Mental Health with Your Employer," on hbr.org, July 30, 2021 (product #H06I2I).

What I didn't know then is that up to 80% of people will experience a diagnosable mental health condition over the course of their lifetime, whether they know it or not.[1] The prevalence of symptoms is the same from the C-suite to individual contributors, but almost 60% of employees have never spoken to anyone at work about their mental health status.[2] Many high performers, including anxious achievers like myself, have strengths that often result from these challenges. I was not nearly as alone as I thought.

Mental health is a spectrum that we all go back and forth on, just like physical health. Most of us fluctuate between stress, burnout, and diagnosable conditions like depression or anxiety, depending on what's happening in our lives. While it may feel harder to disclose bipolar disorder than burnout, everyone should be able to relate on some level.

This has never been truer than it was during the Covid-19 pandemic, when people were dealing with the stressors of the crisis, racial trauma, and more. Managers, direct reports, and colleagues were more vulnerable and authentic than ever due to shared societal challenges and remote work's blurring of the personal and professional. We've also benefited from the courage of public figures who have talked openly about their mental health, such as gymnast Simone Biles, tennis star Naomi Osaka, and Prince Harry and Meghan Markle, the Duchess of Sussex. Not only did they choose to share their challenges, but they also made difficult decisions that put their well-being first.

That said, the effects of stigma can loom large. My self-stigma told me that I was weak and should be ashamed of my anxiety and depression. Societal stigma told me that I would be judged and that professional repercussions would follow if people learned about my condition. However, after widely disclosing it in recent years, none of those things have happened. As a result of my experiences, I founded Mind Share Partners, a non-profit that focuses on changing the culture of workplace mental health. Here's what we recommend if you're considering disclosing a mental health challenge at work.

Reflect on what you're feeling

First, consider what you're experiencing and what the impact is—on your work performance, demeanor, and other factors. What is the duration of the impact? Is it a short blip that will go away in a few days, a longer but episodic challenge, or a chronic condition? Think through what caused your symptoms if they aren't always present. Was it work related, something in your personal life, or a macro stressor?

For me, these elements were clear with minimal self-reflection. I had started a new job with a short-staffed team several months prior. I was unable to do everything asked of me for the first time in my life. On top of that, I had gone off my anxiety medication and was unable to see my therapist regularly because of my new commute. Given everything, I should have been seeing her more often. I had gone from being a high-performing, cheerful colleague to a far-from-competent, aloof individual. It didn't take much for me to put it all together. That said, others may have more complicated narratives that would benefit from discussion with family, friends, or a therapist.

Consider the context and resources

I wish that I'd decided to share enough to get an accommodation right away, or that my organization had promoted flexibility so that I wouldn't even need one. Asking for an accommodation can be scary or nerve-racking, depending on your feelings, your boss, company culture, and other factors. But all I needed from my employer was permission to see my therapist during the workday, which my long commute made tricky. This would have meant coming in late once a week or working from home on Fridays, the latter of which was permitted for employees only after their first six months. However, given my self-stigma and unfounded fear of what my manager might think, I didn't pursue this accommodation. I sometimes wonder how things would have turned out if I'd attributed my need to leave the office to a physical health requirement like a weekly allergy shot.

At the time, workplace mental health wasn't on anyone's radar. No one talked about it openly or had trainings on how to navigate it at work. Now, there are more likely to be clear indicators of whether your company, HR team, or manager supports mental health.

First, consider your company's culture. Have leaders spoken about mental health? Does your company offer workplace mental health trainings? Is there an employee resource group (ERG) for mental health?

Next, think about whether your manager is a safe, supportive person for you. Have they talked about their own mental health or shared other personal challenges?

This level of authenticity builds trust and can be telling. Consider whether your manager has modeled mentally healthy behaviors—even simple things such as exercising regularly, sleeping enough, and taking vacation time. This can help you decide who to share with and how much to disclose.

Then, educate yourself about the protections and benefits you're legally entitled to as an employee. In the United States, for example, businesses with 15 or more employees are required by law to provide reasonable accommodations.[3] Resources and legal protections vary by region, so check your local regulations if possible. This way, you can advocate for yourself if your manager or HR falls short.

Finally, think through the resources or support that would be helpful to you, whether it's access to mental health care, a formal accommodation, or something simpler. Who "owns" this resource? It may be HR, your manager, or someone else.

Explore your comfort level

How much are you comfortable sharing? How much do you actually need to share to achieve your goal? It could be as much detail as your diagnosis and history if you're especially close with your manager. Or, it could be as little as, "I've been having a hard time because of [a general situation in your life]. Is it OK if I take Monday and Tuesday off?"

As a new hire, still trying to prove myself and terrified of professional repercussions, I hadn't wanted to share anything about my anxiety diagnosis up front. However, by sharing only a little I likely could have achieved my goal of having flexible work hours to go to therapy appointments.

If you're not comfortable speaking with your manager, you may prefer to speak with HR or another manager. It's important to have a sense of psychological safety with whomever you choose. Note that your direct manager is typically required to share with HR any employee health information that impacts work—not to be punitive, but to ensure consistency across managers and access to the full array of resources.

Consider in more detail what specific resources or solutions for flexible work you think would be most helpful. You may want to have these ready to name in your conversation. Examples include everything from routine therapy appointments to more frequent check-ins to off-line hours or protected time to focus on work.

If you're like me, you'll also want to turn to safe spaces for input. Since I was already in the throes of anxiety and depression when I decided to disclose, my cognition didn't allow me to problem-solve or make decisions like normal. So, I brainstormed everything with my husband, parents, and therapist. Others might turn to a trusted colleague, a friend, or an ERG for mental health, neuro-diversity, or disability.

Start the conversation

Once you've decided whom to share your experience with, set up a time to talk one-on-one in private. Budget more time than you think you'll need so that the conversation isn't cut short. Be clear about the impact your mental health challenges are having at work. If the cause is work related, share that also.

As much as possible, come with suggestions for how your manager or HR can help you. Have ideas about what changes or resources you'd find beneficial. These can range widely. Examples include: "I'm doing fine now, but it'd be helpful to know what resources are available if I ever need them," or "A conversation about working styles could help set some clarity around our norms and relieve stress." This simple practice of sharing what you and your team members need to do your best work is often all that's necessary. Always feel free to suggest cocreating a solution with your manager and HR—this should ideally be a team effort.

Just as you hope that your manager or HR team will have empathy for you, try to also have empathy for them. While you may have thought about all of this in great detail, it is probably news to them. They may not get everything right in the conversation, but they likely have good intentions. Give them grace and allow them to take some time to circle back with next steps. Be sure to set a time to follow up.

Going forward, I hope that companies and managers make it easier for employees to disclose their mental health challenges and cocreate solutions to ensure that they thrive. I hope that we embrace the opportunity to continue to be vulnerable and authentic at work, as the pandemic necessitated. Rather than saying, "I'm fine," let's give the full, honest answer to "How are you?" We're all dealing with something, however big or small. We just need to let each other know.

Kelly Greenwood is the founder and CEO of Mind Share Partners, a nonprofit that is changing the culture of workplace mental health so that both employees and organizations can thrive. It provides training and strategic advising to leading companies, hosts communities to support ERGs and professionals, and builds public awareness. Kelly has learned to manage her generalized anxiety disorder, which has twice led to debilitating depression. She founded Mind Share Partners to create the resources that she wished she, her managers, and her organization had had when she was struggling. Follow her on Twitter @KellyAGreenwood.

NOTES

1. Jonathan D. Schaefer et al., "Enduring Mental Health: Prevalence and Prediction," *Journal of Abnormal Psychology* 126, no. 2 (2017): 212–224, https://pubmed.ncbi.nlm.nih.gov/27929304/.

2. Mind Share Partners, *Mental Health at Work* 2019 Report, 2019, https://www.mindsharepartners.org/mentalhealthatworkreport.

3. "The ADA: Your Responsibilities as an Employer," U.S. Equal Employment Opportunity Commission, https://www.eeoc.gov/publications/ada-your-responsibilities-employer.

CHAPTER 2

Discussing Your Mental Health with Your Boss

by Deborah Grayson Riegel

When I started my first job, I worried about disclosing my struggle with obsessive-compulsive disorder (OCD) to my boss. I was almost certain that she wouldn't understand. Once she knew, I told myself, she'd assume I was unreliable and uncommitted. I imagined she'd deem me unworthy of a promotion or, worse, be dismissive.

For two months, I ruminated about how the conversation would play out, envisioning every negative outcome. Eventually, I came to this: If I didn't talk to my boss, I wouldn't be able to ask for the support I wanted.

Adapted from "Should You Talk to Your Boss About Your Mental Health?," on hbr.org, September 7, 2021.

So, one day I mustered up the courage, and contrary to my fears, she was empathetic and reassuring. Slowly, I began opening up to my peers and colleagues. I learned that I wasn't the only one living and working with a mental illness.

Looking back, it's surprising that I believed my experience was unique. Nearly 1 billion people in the world live with a mental health disorder, including 47 million Americans.[1] And during the Covid-19 pandemic, symptoms of anxiety and depression rose in the United States—around 80% of people aged 18 to 24 reported moderate to severe symptoms.[2]

Still, discussing mental health in professional settings has long come with stigma. The problem is that when we deliberately avoid addressing mental health at work, that stigma grows. Breaking this cycle often starts by acknowledging our struggles.

When we do (and research confirms this) we are likely to be happier, less stressed, and more confident and productive in our jobs. Opening up can even nudge others to share their experiences—creating a more trusting, psychologically safe, and inclusive space for everyone.

That said, while there are many positives to speaking up at work, doing so can be difficult to navigate—especially for those of us who are new to a job or just beginning our careers.

You may decide not to share if you've previously heard your manager minimize or denigrate mental health or even health in general. You might choose not to disclose to your manager if they've said something like, "Work is about work, not your personal life"—or if the culture reinforces that. You may also choose to keep your mental health status to yourself if your manager has previously shared other people's confidential information.

So, remember: Never pressure yourself to disclose if you're not ready. If you feel you have more to lose than to gain, or need more time to come to a decision, don't force it (and be patient with yourself along the way).

Here are some things to keep in mind when, and if, you feel ready to have this conversation.

Understand what you're disclosing

First, identify whether you're experiencing a mental health challenge or a diagnosed mental health disorder.

A mental health challenge takes place when there's a major change in your thoughts, feelings, or behaviors that interferes with your ability to work or live your life as usual. It may be temporary if it is triggered by a specific event. For instance, a trigger could be social isolation, discrimination or bullying at work, a recent breakup, or a sick family member.

A diagnosed mental health disorder, on the other hand, is often long-lasting and formally diagnosed by a medical or mental health professional. It may disrupt your ability to work, carry out daily activities, or engage in satisfying relationships. Examples include depression, anxiety disorder, post-traumatic stress disorder, and bipolar disorder.

Pay attention to your symptoms and how they impact your day-to-day functioning. If you're having a hard time getting work done, sleeping well, or interacting with others, it might be a sign to seek help—from a professional, as well as at work.

Even if you recognize that your condition is temporary—such as sadness associated with a recent breakup—know that many people benefit from some support. Reflect on what has worked well for you during past mental health setbacks: Speaking with a close friend or family member? Attending a support group for people experiencing similar challenges? Talking to a professional?

Lastly, know that you don't have to share your struggles if you don't feel comfortable doing so.

Think about your "why"

Before disclosing your challenge or disorder, think about what outcome you want. Are you sharing information to build trust with your manager and team? Do you have specific requests that you would like your employer to meet? Is your goal to better understand the workplace policies around mental health?

For instance, if you are facing a mental health challenge, such as stress from taking care of a sick parent, you could plan to tell your manager what you are experiencing. In this case, you may think about requesting some time off or letting your boss know that you'll need to step out of meetings if an emergency arises.

If you are disclosing a longer-term mental health disorder, your goal might be to ask for more permanent accommodations. For example, if you are dealing with a disorder that impacts your concentration, you might request a quiet workspace or a more flexible schedule.

Either way, you should be clear on what you want and why before the conversation.

Know your rights

Before you approach your boss, know that you are not required to share your medical record with anyone. Only refer to the details that you are comfortable telling, or that you feel are relevant to your performance and well-being at work.

You may be entitled to certain legal rights in your city, country, or organization. Take the time to read about the local laws on disability protection and mental health, which you can find by doing an internet search for your location and "disability rights." You'll also want to learn about the policies in your organization. You may want to ask your HR team for additional information if you feel comfortable doing so and trust the team to keep your request confidential.

Many protections around workplace disabilities include mental health disorders. For instance, if you have a U.S. employer, it is illegal for the company to fire you, modify the terms of your contract (including your salary and benefits), or withhold opportunities like promotions, transfers, and professional development programs from you for disclosing your mental health conditions.

Prepare to share your experience

You might have been living with depression, anxiety, OCD, or another mental health challenge or disorder for years. But remember, this could all be new to your boss.

Even if they are familiar with your experience—either personally or by association—it doesn't mean they understand you, your experience, and your unique needs. So, come to the conversation ready to share what your challenge or disorder means and doesn't mean for *you*.

Explain to your manager that each person's experience with mental health is unique. For example, you might say, "I have OCD. For me, that looks like invasive thoughts that can affect my focus at work. When I'm triggered, I have a hard time focusing on a project for more than an hour at a time."

Educating your manager also means being open to their questions. But know that you are allowed to set boundaries when questions feel too intrusive or personal. If you disclose that you're in recovery for a substance abuse disorder, for instance, you might be willing to share that you regularly attend Narcotics Anonymous meetings. However, if they ask about what substances you've used in the past, and their question feels like it's crossing a line, all you need to say is, "I'm not comfortable sharing that."

While you don't have to talk about topics that feel too personal, you can always assure your manager that you have resources in place to support you outside of work (if this is true). That way, they understand that it's not their job to be your counselor or therapist.

Tell your manager what you need

If you're looking for support from your manager and team, make a clear request.

You might say, "I take medication in the morning to help me manage my ADHD. It doesn't really take effect until 10 a.m. So, if you have something to discuss with me that really needs my focus, I would appreciate us scheduling those meetings after 10 so I can be fully present."

You can also reassure your manager that you will reach out for help if needed. You can say, "When I'm taking medication, I can sometimes get a bad headache. I know you and the team care about me—and I promise to proactively share what I need and how I'm doing if I'm not feeling well. How does that sound?"

I also recommend asking your manager or HR department whether your organization offers the following benefits:

- Access to an employee assistance program (EAP), a confidential workplace service that employers pay for and that provides free counseling for employees

- Health insurance with no or low out-of-pocket costs for mental health care

- Free or subsidized coaching, counseling, or self-management programs

- Workshops on stress management and mental well-being

- Quiet workspaces or headsets if you're going to the office

- Extended paid time off or sabbatical leave for mental health reasons

Reinforce helpful behaviors

When you disclose information about your mental health, it's likely that your boss will feel concerned—about you, the team, the workload, and even themselves.

Ensure that you give them regular feedback on what's working and what's not. Acknowledge their small gestures and reinforce behaviors that are helpful to you. This not only will improve your relationships and work environment, but may also help others feel more comfortable opening up about themselves.

For instance, you can say, "When you asked me whether you were overstepping by suggesting I take a day off, I really appreciated that. It felt like you cared about me and how you could be most helpful. Thank you. Also, you were not overstepping. It was just what I needed!"

Ideally, being honest with your boss will help you both create a plan that satisfies your mutual needs. However, if your manager or company culture promotes an "always-on" mentality or doesn't appreciate your vulnerability, it may be a sign of a toxic relationship or workplace.

Talking about your mental health at work shouldn't become an additional stressor for you. If you find yourself in a situation where it's hard to engage with senior leaders about your well-being, it may be time to look for opportunities at organizations that value your whole, authentic self. While it is the responsibility of the employer to create conditions that make you feel safe and valued, the reality is we often have to take the initiative to get what we need.

A job is just a job. No project, deadline, or meeting is worth sacrificing your physical and mental health. It is possible to be an effective and productive employee while still taking care of yourself.

———————

Deborah Grayson Riegel is a keynote speaker, executive coach, and consultant who has taught leadership communication for Wharton Business School, Columbia Business School's Women in Leadership Program, and the Beijing International MBA Program at Peking University. She is the coauthor of *Go to Help: 31 Ways to Offer, Ask for, and Accept Help* and *Overcoming Overthinking: 36 Ways to Tame Anxiety for Work, School, and Life*, both written with her daughter Sophie, a mental health advocate. Deborah has obsessive-compulsive disorder, generalized anxiety disorder, and a tic disorder, and is delighted that she has achieved mental well-being in the face of mental illness.

NOTES

1. "World Mental Health Day: An Opportunity to Kick-Start a Massive Scale-up in Investment in Mental Health," World Health Organization, August 7, 2020, https://www.who.int/news/item/27 -08-2020-world-mental-health-day-an-opportunity-to-kick-start-a -massive-scale-up-in-investment-in-mental-health; "Adult Data 2021," Mental Health America, https://www.mhanational.org/issues/2021/ mental-health-america-adult-data#two.

2. "The State of Mental Health in America," Mental Health America, https://www.mhanational.org/issues/state-mental-health -america.

Caring for Your Mental Health

CHAPTER 3

Structuring the Workday to Support Your Mental Health

by Alice Boyes

When you're struggling with your mental health, getting through your workday can feel a lot harder than usual. If your workload is making your anxiety, depression, or other mental health difficulties worse, it's not always the quantity or type of work that's the culprit. Sometimes it's that your workday isn't structured in a way that suits your natural rhythms or your mental health challenges.

Structuring your workday well can help with a wide range of difficulties, from depression and anxiety to

ADHD and bipolar disorder. But there's no one-size-fits-all version of a mentally healthy workday. What's right for you will be based on self-knowledge, experimentation, and balancing your needs with the needs of others.

How can you figure out the best approach for you? First, I'll describe some specific strategies tied to particular mental health challenges; then I'll discuss mentally healthy time management in general.

Strategies for Specific Mental Health Challenges

Let's start with some advice that may help people who deal with common mental health issues.

Anxiety and depression

Whether your anxiety or depression is chronic or short term, it can make you more likely to avoid certain situations and prone to procrastination. For example, you may find yourself feeling extra sensitive to any signs someone is not happy with your work, but you may also avoid addressing it rather than tackling it head-on. If this sounds like you, consider structuring your days to make avoidance and procrastination more difficult. For example, create short deadlines for steps in a project rather than one deadline for the whole thing. Or, have a set time of day when you take at least one small step forward with a task you're avoiding. Making progress on tasks you'd prefer to avoid will stop the stress from getting even worse.

ADHD

Many mental health challenges cause people to struggle more with planning and seeing the big picture. This is temporary in the case of problems like depression, but more chronic with issues like ADHD. If you feel over-whelmed with planning, try to enlist the assistance of others, when they're willing. For example, ask a client to map out deadlines for each stage of a project, or make planning with others a consistent part of your schedule.

Bipolar disorder

Some folks with mood disorders, especially bipolar dis-order, struggle a great deal when their rhythms are dis-rupted—for example, if you're asked to do shift work or to take an early-morning flight to a conference. If you need a consistent schedule for your mental health, con-sider asking your boss what adaptations are possible.

Any mental health condition

You'll find many examples of the accommodations you can ask for in the United States by searching online or looking at the Equal Employment Opportunity Commis-sion's website.[1] (For more resources you might find use-ful, see this book's introduction.) Anyone with a mental health challenge of any sort should familiarize them-selves with these options.

If you deal with a mental health condition regularly, look into the options available under the Americans with Disabilities Act sooner rather than later—and well before you're in a crisis. Don't make the mistake of thinking your issue doesn't warrant accommodations if it objectively does. And note that different countries use different terms for similar legislation. For example, the United States uses "accommodations," whereas the U.K. uses the phrase "reasonable adjustments."

If you're comfortable, talk to your manager about your condition and why a particular accommodation would be useful to you. Your therapist can help communicate only relevant information without excessive personal details. For example, they could write a letter to your boss to ensure you're comfortable with what they are disclosing.

In general, when you have a mental health difficulty, try not to be constantly overchallenged, but don't completely avoid challenges and triggers either. For example, if you have social anxiety, then sprinkle activities that trigger your anxiety among activities you feel confident with. (For me personally, this means working with people I know well most of the time but working with new collaborators some of the time.)

Strategies That Anyone Can Use

The following steps can help anyone support their mental health at work, whether they deal with a condition chronically, occasionally, or somewhere in between. These strategies also work for people who have subclinical problems (for example, a degree of anxiety but not enough to have been diagnosed with an anxiety disorder) or people seeking to increase their resilience against mental health difficulties or relapses. If you have an active mental illness, including high-functioning depression or anxiety, note that self-care and time management aren't substitutes for actual evidence-based treatments. The strategies mentioned here are supportive; they are not treatments.

Build strong habits around deep work

Developing strong habits around how you work—including how you do deep, focused work—will help you feel in control of your life and schedule.

Why? Consistent routines add structure to our days, boosting our sense of control. Our brains get accustomed to performing sequences of behaviors and eventually start to do these almost on autopilot. A common example of how behaviors become automatic: Within a few months of learning to drive, we all turn on our car, put on our seat belt, release the brake, then look in our mirrors—without really thinking about it. The same thing will happen with your productivity habits if you're consistent with when and where you do your job. If you do deep, focused work during the same slot in your day, like 10 a.m. to noon, keeping up that habit will become easier and more automatic over time, even on days when you're not at your best.

But this will only happen if you've got well-established, consistent habits. If you sometimes do your focused work at 10 a.m., but other times you try to do it at 1 p.m., you won't experience the full benefits of how habits reduce your need for discipline.

Anyone can benefit from this strategy, but particularly those who have episodic mental health challenges, like depression, or those who go through periods when their concentration is poor due to anxiety and rumination or worry. If you have strong habits for when you focus on work, it's more likely you'll get your work done. Keeping up your important habits during stressful times can protect you against the risk of unraveling. It can help you feel steady, stop your confidence from eroding, and ensure you don't have added stress from piles of undone work.

Create routines to do tasks without imminent deadlines

Tackling tasks with imminent deadlines may feel intuitive and obvious, but if all you're getting done is what's right in front of you, you'll generally feel a lack of control. When you accomplish important small tasks that don't have deadlines but that do need to get done, on the other hand, you'll feel like you're managing your life well.

Regularly set aside time for these kinds of small administrative tasks. Whether it's getting back to a colleague about a collaboration that's weeks away or finally scheduling that appointment with the doctor or therapist, admin tasks create a lot of mental drain. You think *I should do that* but don't. And those thoughts keep recurring. To-dos that roll over from one day's list to the next don't feel good.

In my book *Stress-Free Productivity*, I observed that I can do up to an hour of admin tasks before I start my deep work, without disrupting how much deep work I get done. The reason I focus on my admin tasks first is that if I attempt to get to them after deep work, I'm too tired. And checking off at least one "life admin" task (something not related to work) per day keeps them from piling up and creating mental clutter and stress.

Your work and your patterns of attacking it might be different from mine. What's important is that you observe your patterns and sequence tasks accordingly. For example, say that realistically you're only productive for four days a week. Consider accepting that rather than fighting it. If you notice that all you manage to do on Fridays is phone it in, see what happens if you're honest about it. Experiment with organizing your schedule accordingly—get your must-dos done Monday to Thursday—rather than criticizing yourself for the limitations of your focus and discipline. Accepting our limitations can sometimes have a paradoxical effect: Self-criticism takes up a lot of energy, so when we stop doing it, we have more energy for more productive things.

Use an unfocused mind to get things done

A huge part of why work can feel so overwhelming is the false idea that we should be focused and undistracted all day. That's not possible, and not necessary or desirable, especially if you're trying to do anything innovative.

It's more realistic and mentally healthier to have a mind that's alternately focused and unfocused, because during our brains' unfocused recovery time we make creative connections without even trying to. For example, you've probably had a brilliant idea for a project while taking a shower or going for a walk, right? When we're unfocused, pathways that felt murky while we were concentrating can suddenly become clear.

Problems we couldn't solve from up close up suddenly become simpler.

So rather than trying to force your brain to do task after task, let it relax and wander after you've been productive for a while. Personally, I achieve this through a combination of walks, errands, chores around the house, and entertainment (like reading a blog post in the middle of the workday).

I need to let my mind wander most after deep work sessions or when I'm feeling overwhelmed by how to prioritize. If I take a walk when I'm feeling mentally cluttered, my unfocused mind usually does my prioritizing and organizing for me. If you're stuck on an assignment and aren't sure what to do next, rather than stressing about it, let your mind wander for a bit. That way you'll be able to mull over ideas without just staring at a blank page.

Unfocused time can also be hugely helpful to people experiencing mental health challenges at work. For example, someone with social anxiety needs breathing space to recover from feedback or to adjust to the working styles of new collaborators. Likewise, someone with depression needs opportunities for small bites of pleasure, like a leisurely coffee in a sunny spot, to bolster their mood.

Making time to be unfocused should become a regular part of your habits. Maybe you can do your deep work in the mornings and then treat your afternoons as opportunities for serendipity and wandering. However you do it, find ways to let your brain off the hook for a while each day. And remember, the more you're doing novel or innovative work, the more you'll need mental down-time to recover from the toll of it. Very challenging work involves lots of mental and emotional fallout, including disappointment, uncertainty, and frustration. If you expect yourself to be firing on all cylinders at all times, you'll shy away from doing the types of novel and challenging work that require unfocused recovery time.

What Managers Need to Know

If you're a manager, make sure you understand how the previous advice will help your staff both feel better and do their work better, and familiarize yourself with the types of accommodations that help people with specific mental health challenges. You can do this by simply searching online, talking to HR, or asking a psychologist to do an education session for your workplace. With the latter option, explain to the psychologist in advance how your workplace functions so they can consider types of flexibility that won't be excessively disruptive.

Learn from your staff about what their difficulties are and what would help them, and of course, never judge them negatively for their mental health. A particular difficulty doesn't say anything about their talent, dedication, or their quality of work. Since people may be reluctant to ask for accommodations, remind staff regularly that you're open to requests and that you welcome honest conversations about mental illness and health. Be as creative as you can in making accommodations. Your job is to bring out the best in your people, and you'll do that by supporting their mental health in the ways they request.

Structuring your workday to support your mental health and structuring it to do your best work don't have to be at odds. Using the tips from this chapter, you should see improvements in both your mental well-being and your productivity.

––––––––––––

Alice Boyes is a former clinical psychologist turned author. Writing her first book, *The Anxiety Toolkit*, a *Wall Street Journal* bestseller, helped her develop a positive view of her own anxious personality. Her latest book is *Stress-Free Productivity*. Alice blogs for *Psychology Today* and hbr.org.

NOTE

1. "Depression, PTSD, & Other Mental Health Conditions in the Workplace: Your Legal Rights," U.S. Equal Employment Opportunity Commission, https://www.eeoc.gov/laws/guidance/depression-ptsd -other-mental-health-conditions-workplace-your-legal-rights.

CHAPTER 4

Managing Your Anxiety

by Charlotte Lieberman

When I was nine, I was diagnosed with an anxiety disorder by my first-ever therapist. My parents dragged me into treatment after repeatedly catching me cleaning their bathroom. I didn't mind, but I was confused. I didn't see anything wrong with what I was doing: organizing their medicine cabinet by color and size, throwing out expired antibiotics and sticky bottles of cough syrup. My favorite part was wiping down the sink with warm water, feeling my worries wash away with stubble and soap scum. Cleaning gave me the sense that I could find inner order among the outer chaos—our cramped

---

Adapted from "How to Manage Your Anxiety," on hbr.org, September 18, 2020.

New York apartment, murmurs of my parents' struggling marriage, the growing pains of adolescence.

Now, two decades later, I still rely on cleaning as a coping mechanism for my anxiety. My therapist encourages me to "sit with the feeling" instead, and sometimes I can tolerate it. There are mornings when I can wake up, take a shower, and go about my day with relative ease. There are also mornings when I feel imprisoned in a labyrinth of negative thoughts. Taking walks helps. Placing a heating pad on my stomach does too. For now, I am sitting with my anxiety, drinking my morning coffee, reminding myself to be grateful for my support system and the tools that help me manage.

It's all a practice.

Based on my personal experience and research, I've learned there's no one-size-fits-all method for determining when anxiety becomes maladaptive and when to get help. The fact is that anxiety exists at different levels and in different ways in each of us, depending on our brain chemistry, genetic makeup, background, environment, social relationships, and so on.

Across the board, anxiety becomes problematic when it feels unmanageable—which also means different things for different people. Perhaps its intensity gets in the way of your day-to-day functioning. Maybe the feeling is so diffuse and unspecific that you feel at a loss for how to address it, and wondering only sucks you deeper into a quicksand of anxious thoughts. You might find yourself fixating on something that you know isn't a cause for worry, but you still can't help it. These are just some of the signs that you might benefit from professional mental health support. I know I have.

Whether on your own or alongside a therapist (I recommend both), the key to managing anxiety is learning to identify it, understand it, and respond to it with self-compassion. I'll share a few research-based practices that can, hopefully, help you cope more skillfully with anxiety, no matter what it looks like for you.

Get to know your anxiety

From the wellness industry to tech and beyond, capitalism has influenced how we think about even our most mortal problems. Hunger, thirst, fatigue, boredom: There's an app for all of it. But framing anxiety as a "problem" that needs a quick fix can kick-start a vicious fight-or-flight cycle. When we view our painful emotions as a threat to fight or flee from, we turn ourselves into the enemy. So, rather than working against ourselves and trying to resist or run away from negative feelings, what if we learned to approach them with kindness?

Research shows that mindfulness techniques like breath work can reduce anxiety and improve cognition.[1] They help us tap into the region of our brains responsible for awareness, concentration, and decision making (the prefrontal cortex), and put us in a calmer, more focused state. We are able to think more clearly and make better, more thoughtful decisions, rather than relying on the part of our brains that views anxiety as a threat (the amygdala).

The next time you're spiraling—whether about work or your partner or nothing at all—pause and imagine anxiety knocking at your front door. Tell it, "One minute!" Then give yourself a moment to pause and try this breathing cycle: Inhale for four seconds, hold for four seconds, exhale for four seconds, hold for four seconds. This technique is known as box breathing, and it is a fast, effective way to calm the nervous system by tricking the mind into believing that the body is relaxed.

Once you've calmed down, imagine opening your front door and saying, "Ah, anxiety. Thanks for coming, but I'm not free right now."

The goal is to gently create distance between you, your thoughts, and your emotions. Pinpointing where in your body the uncomfortable feelings reside can also help. Are they a tightness in your chest, or a churning in your stomach? Simply notice. By taking a step back from your discomfort, you may be able to relate to it with a bit more clarity. You gain the relief of perspective: *This is an uncomfortable experience. This is not* me.

Choose an anchor

Routines help reduce general feelings of anxiety and are often effective antidotes for those with more serious mental health disorders. Doing the same thing at regular intervals signals to our brains that we are safe. Call it a routine, a ritual, an anchor—whatever resonates.

For me, writing three pages in my journal every morning is nonnegotiable. This means I do it whether I feel like it or not, and knowing that I can follow through on this task—no matter what—gives me a reliable well of self-trust that I can dip into whenever anxiety tugs. Plus, writing down my thoughts is a cathartic, ground-ing exercise in and of itself. And it's not just true for me: Journaling is often used as a therapeutic tool for people with anxiety and other mental health conditions.

Whatever routine you choose, make it a formal commitment. If it helps to keep you accountable, tell a colleague, friend, or partner about your routine, and ask them to check in with you weekly. Maybe write it on a sticky note and put it on your laptop. But don't make it a chore.

You may find you feel a greater sense of safety and comfort once you apply this practice. And when you fall off the wagon, try to forgive yourself and move on.

Reframe self-discipline as a form of kindness

We are often conditioned to believe that feeling like our "best self" results from maintaining a laundry list of self-care practices. But for those of us with anxiety, self-care can actually be a major source of stress. My anxiety lends itself to perfectionism, which means I instinctively shudder at the thought of adding anything to my plate.

I long resisted the benefits of exercise, avoided having a social life, and dismissed my hobbies simply because I felt overwhelmed by the idea not just of having more to do but of having to do it perfectly. After work, I'd come home, eat takeout, and scroll on Instagram until my eyes fluttered shut. This, I rationalized, was self-care. Except that it made me feel terrible.

With time and the help of my therapist, I eventually learned to adopt a different attitude. Yes, self-care requires a degree of discipline. But discipline can be kind.

Yoga and meditation are two ways to practice what I call "supportive discipline." Focusing on the breath—and gently releasing distractions as they arise—requires both kindness and discipline. In Buddhism, this key tenet is roughly translated as "right effort." As a meditation teacher once explained to me, you can think of your breath as a fragile object: If you grip it too tightly, it will break. But if you completely slacken your hand, it will fall. This practice of finding and maintaining that careful balance, to me, is a great image of supportive discipline.

Of course, meditation doesn't feel great for everyone—and that's OK. There are an infinite number of ways to practice being kinder to yourself and tuning into the present moment. You could try new hobbies like brewing beer, crocheting, rollerblading, beekeeping. Exercising, drawing, and listening to music are evidence-based ways to reduce anxiety and regulate emotions. Find what works for you. Then do it. Period.

Visualize positive change

In the midst of anxiety, finding motivation to do *anything* can be the trickiest part. Try to connect to the positive feeling that will result from taking the action that feels hard, whether that's going for a run or getting out of bed in the morning. Simply imagining success is correlated with feeling motivated and achieving goals.[2]

When you're imagining how good it will feel, whatever "it" is, encourage yourself as you would a good friend. There is a robust body of recent research on the mental health benefits of "self-distancing," which researchers compare to "the experience of seeking out a friend's counsel on a difficult problem."[3] Rather than becoming "immersed" in the painful, often paralyzing feeling of anxiety, we can momentarily envision ourselves offering guidance to a good friend. *Stretch. Make fruit salad. Watch a romantic comedy.*

Anxiety is stubborn, so you'll likely try to wriggle out of the good advice your "distanced" self is giving. But try to engage in the mental role play as best as you can. "Whereas it is often challenging for the person experiencing a personal dilemma to reason objectively about their own circumstances," researchers explain, "friends are often uniquely capable of providing sage advice because they're not involved in the experience."[4]

Imagine that! What would it feel like *not* to be involved in the experience of anxiety? Be creative.

Simple as these tips are, they may not always feel easy. They certainly don't for me. If anxiety is good for anything, it is making simple things feel complicated and insurmountable.

The bottom line? We can choose to be kinder, patient, and more compassionate with ourselves. Uncomfortable feelings will persist and subside—then persist again. The most productive thing any of us can do is show up for ourselves and others with open minds and hearts. It may not be the first priority on your to-do list, but let it be enough.

––––––––––––

Charlotte Lieberman is a multidisciplinary writer and marketing consultant for wellness and health-care brands. She is also a certified hypnotherapist and coach and has developed a compassion-based practice informed by research and personal experience with anxiety. Charlotte's work has been featured on *CBS This Morning*, *The TODAY Show*, and NPR, and she frequently speaks about mental health and mindfulness at organizations.

NOTES

1. Michael Christopher Melnychek et al., "Coupling of Respiration and Attention via the Locus Coeruleus: Effects of Meditation and Pranayama," *Psychophysiology* 55, no. 9 (2018), https://onlinelibrary.wiley.com/doi/abs/10.1111/psyp.13091.

2. Tim Blankert and Melvyn R. W. Hamstra, "Imagining Success: Multiple Achievement Goals and the Effectiveness of Imagery," *Basic and Applied Social Psychology* 39, no. 1 (2017): 60–67, https://www.ncbi.nlm.nih.gov/pmc/articles/PMC5351796/.

3. E. Kross and O. Ayduk, "Self-Distancing: Theory, Research, and Current Directions," *Advances in Experimental Social Psychology*, 2016, http://selfcontrol.psych.lsa.umich.edu/wp-content/uploads/2017/04/SD.pdf.

4. Kross and Ayduk, "Self-Distancing."

CHAPTER 5

Working When You're Depressed

by Alice Boyes

Over the past two years, I've slogged through many, many unsuccessful rounds of fertility treatments while trying to have a second child. To say the stress and grief from this has affected my mood and anxiety levels would be an understatement. It's been hard not to plunge into a deep depression, and I've struggled at times.

Yet I've managed to stay reasonably functional and productive. How? Using tips from my psychology training.

If you're depressed, your number one job is to look after yourself. Productivity is secondary to your mental

---

Adapted from "How to Get Something Done When You're Feeling Down," on hbr.org, October 20, 2021 (product #H06N5O).

health. However, learning how to be productive when you're feeling down can help with depression recovery. If your first reaction to this topic is that it feels like extra pressure, stick with me while I explain how and why being productive can help with depression.

All emotions have an evolved purpose as a signaling system. They let you know whether you're safe or in danger, or whether you're heading in the right or the wrong direction. Sadness, depression, and apathy, for example, cause us to pause, withdraw, and reflect, which has self-protective aspects. Sometimes it's wise to cocoon away from danger. Sometimes it's wise to question what we find meaning in and not to keep plowing ahead doing the same things. But with depression, this withdrawn, low-energy mode essentially gets stuck "on" and becomes unhelpful. Instead of our feelings signaling the need to rethink what we're doing, they make everything start to feel meaningless. When these emotions become prolonged, they lose their effectiveness as signals. The more low energy you are, the less you do, the worse you feel, and the cycle continues. Being productive can help interrupt that negative spiral and turn it around. Here's where to start.

Schedule daily sources of accomplishment and pleasure

For mood health, we need two types of activities: those that provide a sense of accomplishment and those that provide pleasure. A well-researched therapy for depression called behavioral activation is based on this principle.

As a general rule, try to have one source of accomplishment and one source of pleasure in each of your mornings, afternoons, and evenings. (You would end up with six per day—three for pleasure, and three for a sense of accomplishment.) These can be very simple. For example, pleasure could come from sitting in a sunny window to drink your morning coffee. A sense of accomplishment could come from exercising, vacuuming under your bed, or doing a work task. Some people find it helpful to schedule activities in advance so they can more easily do all six.

If you're depressed, the pleasure you get from activities will typically be muted compared to a normal response, so it may be a little harder to identify activities you would enjoy. This is another reason to schedule in advance. Start by brainstorming a list of the activities that provide pleasure or a sense of accomplishment for you. If you feel stuck, ask someone who knows you well to help.

This tip benefits productivity in direct and indirect ways. Activities that provide a sense of accomplishment are productive, and the structure of this approach will benefit your biological rhythms and your mood.

Reduce your usual workload

When you're struggling with your mood and high stress levels, attempting to work at 100% of your usual output is ill advised. However, not working at all typically isn't helpful either. Why?

Regular work helps provide structure to your day. When you have the structure of regular activities, this helps regulate your biological rhythms, such as those related to eating and sleeping. Without the structure of regular activities, including work and socializing, those biological rhythms will become more dysregulated, which will tend to make depression worse.

Fifty percent of your usual activity is a good sweet spot between not working enough and expecting too much of yourself. You may even find that your productivity doesn't decrease that much with this approach, since it will force you to prioritize deep work and other truly important tasks. Limiting yourself to 50% of your usual work will help you let go of activities that were only medium-productive to begin with. Fifty percent isn't a hard and fast rule. You can choose a different number if you'd prefer, but adopt the principle.

Alternate between easy, medium, and hard tasks

Another element of good mood hygiene is not doing all easy tasks or all hard tasks over long stretches of time. You don't need to take my word for this; you can easily observe for yourself how you feel if you are constantly challenged to the edge of your capacities versus if you intersperse hard activities with familiar ones you feel confident with but that still feel meaningful and productive (for example, mowing your lawn or writing your monthly newsletter).

When you're scheduling your three activities per day that will provide a sense of accomplishment, aim for one hard, one easy, and one medium.

Cultivate a deep work habit to reduce your need for self-control

If you're depressed, you'll want to rely on self-control as little as possible, because everything feels harder when your mood is low. The best way to reduce the self-control needed for highly productive work is through strong habits. By this, I mean a daily routine of doing deep work at the same time each day for a couple of hours. A habit you do every weekday at the same time will be easier to keep up than one you do at varying times. This approach also helps reduce decision fatigue. (For more on strong habits, see chapter 3.)

Eventually you'll be able to start deep work on auto-pilot, without it feeling like a big lift. For example, I start my deep work sessions by mixing an electrolyte drink and setting timers for 60, 90, and 120 minutes. (And I don't use my phone for the timer, so my device won't distract me while I'm writing.) Initially I stumbled into this routine, but once it became my habit, I kept it up. My original reason for using the timers was to train myself to concentrate for two-hour blocks, and to help me better understand what the fluctuations in my focus were across my work period. The timers also help me pace myself, avoid unproductive overworking, and avoid boom-and-bust cycles of activity. In addition, I find it harder to concentrate in the second hour and need to be more protective of my concentration then. The timers remind me to do that.

Once firmly established, your habit will become much easier to maintain, no matter what mood you're in.

Consider getting treatment for your mental health

This might sound obvious, but a way to be more productive if you're depressed is not to be depressed anymore or to be less so. Almost universally, people wait far too long before accessing treatment for their mental health. When I was a therapist, I would ask clients when the onset of the problem was. Frequently, the answer would be "years ago," not months or weeks.

There are a variety of approaches you can try, including cognitive-behavioral therapy, acceptance and commitment therapy, or medication. To support your treatment, you might try taking a broad-based multivitamin and mineral supplement to help you be resilient to stress, especially if your eating habits have worsened due to your depression. Learning self-compassion skills can also be extremely beneficial for depression, stress, and anxiety if you tend to be self-critical. Skills for identifying and disrupting rumination are important to master, as rumination impairs mood, productivity, and problem solving.

Treatment can also help you understand how depressed feelings affect your functioning. For example, depressed feelings put people on the lookout for any signs of interpersonal rejection. This is part of their evolved purpose, since in an evolutionary sense, it's dangerous to be excluded from our tribe. In reality, this isn't always helpful. At work, rejection can manifest in perceiving other people as unsupportive, not liking you, or not recognizing your talents and capabilities, even when this isn't the case. And that can lead to misplaced irritability and hostility toward bosses, coworkers, or clients.

When you're depressed or experiencing emotions like grief or anxiety, you won't always be able to be as productive as you'd ideally like. Be patient with yourself, but also give the recommended advice a try. Depression often causes people to have negative expectations, which can include expecting advice not to work for you. If you know this, you can avoid this trap and experiment with the strategies provided.

Alice Boyes is a former clinical psychologist turned author. Writing her first book, *The Anxiety Toolkit*, a *Wall Street Journal* bestseller, helped her develop a positive view of her own anxious personality. Her latest book is *Stress-Free Productivity*. Alice blogs for *Psychology Today* and hbr.org.

CHAPTER 6

Dealing with a Panic Attack

by Ruth C. White

You're at work when you suddenly feel a deep sense of dread. Heart pounding, hands trembling, lightheaded and drenched in sweat, you can't breathe. You think you're having a heart attack and feel like you're about to die. You're about to call for an ambulance when the symptoms start to fade. You just had a panic attack.

What Is a Panic Attack?

The American Psychological Association (APA) describes a panic attack as "a sudden surge of overwhelming fear that comes without warning and without any obvious reason." The feelings and physical symptoms

---

Adapted from "Managing a Panic Attack at Work," on hbr.org, March 21, 2022 (product #H06X5O).

you experience (such as shortness of breath and tightness in your chest) are very real and can be very scary. Panic attacks won't kill you, but depending on how severe and frequent they are, they can have a significant impact on your quality of life. Often triggered by stressful situations, the symptoms of panic attacks usually recede when the stress ends. Common triggers at work include public speaking, conflict, an important meeting, a major transition such as a promotion or a big project, or a work-related social event such as a meeting with a key client or after-work drinks.

Symptoms of a panic attack include the following, according to the APA:

- Racing heart rate

- Shortness of breath

- An almost paralyzing fear

- Dizziness, lightheadedness, or nausea

- Trembling, sweating, or shaking

- Choking or chest pains

- Hot flashes or sudden chills

- Tingling in fingers and toes (pins and needles)

- A fear that you're going to die

Panic attacks are singular events; many people have only one or two in their lives. If you have had more than that, the APA suggests you contact a mental health professional for diagnosis and treatment, because you may have a panic disorder. A panic disorder is a condition in which people have frequent or debilitating fear and anxiety without a reasonable cause, and it may be accompanied by fear of another attack, concern about the impact of these attacks, and a change of behavior in response to them. The persistent fear of future panic attacks is a key symptom of panic disorder and can lead to avoiding the situation that caused the attack—which can be a real problem at work. According to the APA, panic disorders affect approximately 1.3% of the U.S. population. The onset usually begins in adolescence or early adulthood, and although the causes are not clear, major life transitions and stressful social or economic events, such as a pandemic or a market crash, can trigger them. There also is a familial connection: If others in your family have had a panic disorder, you have an increased likelihood of suffering from attacks.

But if you find yourself having occasional or frequent panic attacks, know that they *can* be treated—and the earlier you get treatment, the better. Even if an attack is only your first or second, it's important to seek medical attention when it's over, because the symptoms are similar to those of serious health problems, like a heart attack.

Managing a Panic Attack at Work

We know work can be stressful, so it's not surprising that many people experience panic attacks while on the job. This can add to your stress, because you're not at home where you can lie down on the sofa or curl up on your bed.

When you feel a panic attack coming on, find a quiet, private place to sit until the symptoms pass. If you're in a meeting or another high-pressure situation, try to calmly remove yourself by stepping out to get water or visit the restroom. If you're worried about your absence raising alarms, text a colleague that you're not feeling well and will be back when you feel better. Once you're in quiet space, use the following strategies to manage your symptoms.

1. **Breathe deep and slow.** To try to control your breathing, close your eyes (this reduces stimulation), and focus on taking deep and slow breaths through your mouth. Breathe in for a count of four, hold for a second, and then breathe out for a count of four. This will slow your heart rate and may counteract feelings of dizziness. It will also give you a feeling of control and thus reduce your fear. If you cannot control your breathing, sit down and put your head between your legs, or breathe into a paper bag if you have one.

2. **Try mindfulness.** You are in a heightened emotional state; remind yourself to take long, slow, deep breaths. Focusing on your breath will distract you from your thought patterns. Tell yourself, "I am not dying. This will pass." Bring your attention to the present. Focus on your physical sensations, and name three things you can see, three things you can hear, and three things you can feel. If you practice yoga, a centering yoga pose (like Sukhasana or easy pose) can also bring on a state of mindfulness.

3. **Visualize a peaceful and happy place.** Think about a place that relaxes you: a favorite beach, a hike, a lake. Imagine yourself there and picture as many details as possible. Like the mindfulness exercise, focus on what you can see and hear and feel. Is there sun streaming through the trees or reflecting off the lake? Is there a smell of leaves or flowers? What does the sand feel like between your toes?

4. **Repeat a mantra.** If you already have a mantra or favorite words of affirmation, repeat them. If not, close your eyes and repeat one of the following phrases: "This will pass," or "I will be fine," or "I will get through this."

5. **Take a break.** If you can, tell your boss you're not feeling well and need to step away. Take 15 minutes before going back to your office or your desk. Don't check your phone. Drink a cup of herbal tea. Walk or sit outside. Or if you cannot remove yourself, or don't have 15 minutes, then just sit still for 5 minutes. You may also want to go home for the rest of the day to relax and regroup, if possible. And if this is not your first panic attack, consult with a medical provider.

Helping Someone Who Is Having a Panic Attack

While you shouldn't "diagnose" a panic attack in someone else, learning to recognize the symptoms will help you better support someone who's in distress. When speaking to the person, remain calm and use a calm voice. You can help in the following five ways:

1. **Ask.** Don't assume you know what's going on. Calmly ask if and how they would like your assistance. Say something like, "Miguel, are you OK? Would you like me to go outside with you so you can catch your breath?" If the person seems like they can't communicate and you think they are having a heart attack, then call an ambulance immediately and let medical professionals make the assessment.

2. **Find a quiet, private place.** Reducing environmental stimuli can ease stress and help reduce the effects of dizziness and nausea. Ask your colleague whether they'd like you to help them find somewhere quiet to sit. If they say yes, do so. If they say no, then ask if there is anything you can do to help them. And if they refuse your help, then just let them know you are there for them if they change their mind.

3. **Listen.** Respect boundaries, and if the person is able to say how you can support them, follow their lead. Remember that their response may be curt because they're in emotional distress. They may be ashamed to be experiencing a panic attack in public. If they ask you to leave, let them know that you'll be nearby if they change their mind. Say something like, "I don't want to leave

you alone when you seem so distressed, so I will be nearby to support you if you need me." Then give them some space, but stay close enough to come if they call you.

4. **Reassure.** If the person asks you to stay, tell them that you are there to support them. Introduce a mantra as a way of focusing their attention elsewhere. Suggest they repeat after you, "I am going to be OK." Help them breathe slowly. Model slow and purposeful breathing. Ask them to close their eyes and to breathe along with you, using the method described earlier. Repeat until their breathing slows and they regain control.

After the panic attack passes, reassure your colleague that the experience will not affect the way you think about them at work, and that you will protect their privacy and not share what happened with anyone. (And, of course, do as you promise.) Encourage your colleague to take a few minutes, or the rest of the day, to recover if they're able to.

Sharing About Your Panic Attacks

You don't need to share with your boss or HR that you get panic attacks. However, if you choose to disclose your panic disorder, remember that you get to decide how much you want to share. Disclosure about your panic disorder may be protected under the Americans with Disabilities Act or equivalent, which means that your disclosure cannot be cause for dismissal or demotion. It also means that you may qualify for accommodations, such as taking more breaks. Check with a lawyer to see what applies in your area.

Although panic attacks can be distressing, the implications for how people see you at work can cause additional stress. The strategies described here can help you manage your symptoms and keep them from taking over your workday. Of course, don't neglect to seek out professional support and guidance as well if you need it.

Ruth C. White is a mental health advocate who often shares her journey of recovery and resilience with bipolar disorder in her talks, workshops, and writings. White has authored four books on mental health, including *Bipolar 101: A Practical Guide to Identifying Triggers, Managing Medications, Coping with Symptoms, and More* and *The Stress Management Workbook: De-Stress in 10 Minutes or Less*. She blogs for *Psychology Today*, writes for *Thrive Global*, and appears frequently as a mental health commentator and educator on KRON4 TV Bay Area. For seven years she was a clinical associate professor of social work at the University of Southern California and was a tenured social work professor at Seattle University.

Bringing Our Full Selves to Work

CHAPTER 7

Being an "Only" at the Office

An interview with Angela Neal-Barnett and Nilofer Merchant by Morra Aarons-Mele

Being an "only" or a "first" at work—a minority in the office because of race, background, gender, sexual orientation, or another identity—can seriously impact someone's mental health. To find out how an only can find strength in who they are, Morra Aarons-Mele, host of the HBR podcast *The Anxious Achiever*, spoke with Angela Neal-Barnett, the first Black woman to be tenured and promoted to the rank of professor in the Kent State University Department of Psychological Sciences, where she directs the program for research on anxiety

Adapted from "The Anxiety of Being the 'Only,'" *The Anxious Achiever* podcast, season 1, episode 3, October 14, 2019.

disorders among African Americans, and Nilofer Merchant, the author of *The Power of Onlyness* and a four-time Thinkers50 top management leader.

Morra Aarons-Mele: Angela, your "first" status is loud and proud on your bio, but what has it been like for you to be a first and an only throughout your career?

Angela Neal-Barnett: I'm not going to sugarcoat it. There've been times when it's been really wonderful and times when I thought I should get paid for being Black. So, it's been ups and downs with challenges and triumphs. Sometimes, you don't realize you're an only until it hits you in the face. I had an incident rather recently where somebody said to me, "We just didn't understand the value of your work." And I thought, "I wonder if other people who are an only get that."

You've written, "To fully understand anxiety in Black women, we must understand how Black women are viewed in this country." How are Black women viewed in the United States, and how does this contribute to their anxiety?

There are three major images or views of Black women. Everybody knows the "strong Black woman," the woman who keeps on keeping on, who can handle anything. That's just not a true image. Then there's the "Jezebel," the highly sexualized Black woman stereotype. Finally, there's the "angry Black woman" image we see over and over again.

How do those stereotypes come into play when a Black woman's credentials are on par with everyone else's in the office?

Either people say, "Well, you're not like other Black women," which goes to the idea that people believe there's only one way to be Black in this country. Or they try to fit you into one of those stereotypes. They may see you as the strong Black woman, so when anything happens, they come running to tell you all their problems, because you can help them fix it. But if you assert yourself, then they say, "Oh, we got an angry Black woman in the office."

What are the stakes of failure? When you are an anxious person, you might be a perfectionist, or you might catastrophize failures at work that other people don't even notice. There might be pressure like, "Oh my gosh, if I don't make it, I'm letting myself down and I'm letting a community down." How does that play into anxiety?

"Collectivism" is what it's called. When we do something, it's not only our success; it's the family's success and the community's success. I always tell people that when I received my PhD, 28 other people received it with me. But when you're anxious and you're an only and a first, those three things combine to make the failure feel worse than it actually is.

What do you say to a person who's up for a big promotion and is saying, "If I don't get this, that's it"?

What we say is, "So what?" and try to dig into their anxiety. Because what we're really trying to do is get at their core fear. If we can do that, then we can work to overcome the fear.

Oftentimes in our work with organizations, we find that, at least in the beginning, many Black women are reluctant to do therapy for this kind of anxiety. So we use something called "sister circles." We bring together 4 to 10 Black women and do some exercises to help them recognize and then reduce their anxiety. One example is what I just mentioned, the "so what?" thinking. Many of these women are sharing the same core fear. What they haven't understood is that they aren't the only ones. Then all of a sudden, they find that three other people feel the way they do. They're not alone.

Are there unique challenges that Black women might face if they do get a mental health diagnosis and the workplace knows about it, or if they're in a mental health crisis at work?

In an environment where there's no other Black person, then people might say, "OK, she's having some issues. I'll just let her figure it out." Whereas if it's somebody of the majority race in the workplace who's struggling, people might say, "OK, let's see what we can do to help you."

If a Black woman is having a panic attack or enduring a social situation with social anxiety, it might be misconstrued. So, whenever I see an "angry

Black woman," I always want to assess for social
anxiety, because that anger might be a defense when
having to do the cocktail parties, the small talk, the
fundraisers, the galas, and so on.

Most Black women, particularly those who are in
high-profile positions or who are an only, see themselves as strong Black women; to be weak and a Black
woman is an oxymoron, and mental health crises at
work are a sign of weakness. When you're an only,
your belief is that people are looking for an excuse to
pull you down, to put you down.

**If someone is an ambitious only and thinks, "I want a
sister circle. I need to work on this," what's the first step
they can take to connect with others and address their
anxiety in a real way?**

The first step is just to acknowledge your anxiety. You
have named it, and that is the beginning of understanding. Once you do that, everything else comes
into place. The second thing is to say, "OK, let me
ask for help." Most Black women want help from
someone who understands their issues and looks like
them.

Most HR departments have employee assistance
programs or mental health professionals that they
contract with. You can certainly talk to them and say,
"I'm looking for someone who understands Black
anxiety or the anxiety of the only." There are people
who do specialize in that. And if HR isn't helpful,
a number of organizations, like the Anxiety and

Depression Association of America, can refer you to a therapist in your area who is the same race or is culturally competent.

Nilofer Merchant has another angle on this topic. Nilofer, how do you define onlyness?

Nilofer Merchant: Onlyness is that singular spot in the world where only one stands. It's the source of ideas that, in this modern economy, is also the source of all value creation. I coined the term "onlyness" back in 2011 to shift the narrative, so we could stop talking about differences in a way that subjugates one group. For example, the phrase "difference" usually refers to people of color and women and so on. Actually, every single one of us is different, so we need to stop making one group distinct from everyone else. We need to stop having one group be seen for what they can offer, and one group be seen through the lens of otherness. Onlyness is a way of bridging all that into one term.

Why is onlyness an important concept for ambitious professionals who might struggle with anxiety or depression?

What I probably say to people more than anything else is that for a long time, you've been conditioned to believe that somehow your "difference" is wrong and that you have to overcome some hurdle. I want to say that you're perfectly fine just as you are. The fact that the world can't see you, or doesn't want to see you, is a challenge. But in some ways, it's not about you. We can learn to separate ourselves and our anxiety from who we actually are.

For those of us who have been othered for so long, whether it's because of our sexual orientation, our age, or all the ways in which people can be othered, it means that between 50% and 70% of ideas are lost in the economy at a personal level. That's the irony of originality. While each of us has a distinct perspective, some of us are called "different" when we are each distinctly ourselves. Some of us are constantly seen through a subjective lens, as young or gay or female or whatever, rather than as a subject of our own story. If we're seen through the lens of otherness, we're not actually being seen as ourselves, and therefore the ideas we have are either suppressed to fit in or ignored. This is why otherness hurts innovation. The world of work needs the ideas that we each have to offer.

We're both big fans of the work of Rosabeth Moss Kanter from Harvard Business School, whose research has explored tokenism. When you represent a group that's less than 15% of the total makeup of your organization, you experience othering that can really constrain your ideas. But othering also creates tremendous stress and anxiety in and of itself. If you're visibly different in a workplace, how does being an other diminish your power and how can it create anxiety?

Kanter said, "If you're an only, you're going to get stereotyped." So, you're going to get told, "Oh, women are not ambitious," or "Young people don't know enough." What I found really interesting about her data was to realize that stereotypes are outside our control. So if you're being tokenized and dismissed in the room, go build or get yourself into new rooms.

Part of what Kanter was also talking about is that, when you are the only, you have to be responsible for everyone who's like you. You're the mouthpiece for them in the room you're in. We often talk about how employee resource groups can help people, so they can talk about anxiety and mental health. But I worry that by doing that, even if the ERG is helpful, you become that person with the mental health condition who's willing to talk about it: "I'm the one who's out and proud about having a mental health disorder; I'm the anxious woman in the office."

You're carrying a much bigger load.

Totally. Also, "Is that all I'm known for?" So what does someone do there?

It's totally fine if you end up having anxiety and really care about that issue and want to champion it. But you want to be able to define what matters to you rather than have someone else define it. For example, I was born a woman, I was born brown— aspects of my identity but not my full identity. Are my people women? Are my people brown people? If I was limited by the identities assigned to me rather than an identity I chose, I would miss the opportunity to find or build the rooms where people care about how to grow value creation from typically unheard voices. So the most important thing is to figure out who your people are by defining who you are. Then figure out how to connect to them and support each other.

What is your take on imposter syndrome, and how do you counsel people to think about it if they're experiencing it?

What I think happens is sometimes we walk into a room and the predominant group of engineers behaves *this* way, but we may want to behave another way. Or marketing behaves *that* way, and we don't have that profile. We can feel like imposters when we're behaving the way we think other people expect us to. We've almost walked outside of ourselves to adopt the norms of someone else.

Let's say I'm a guy who cares about actively raising my children. That's something I might have to jettison to adopt the norms of the majority group, since many people don't expect men to be active caregivers. Yet, if you are really celebrating your onlyness, you're going to say, "You know what? I go home at 4:45 because I do daycare pickup. I know it's not the gendered role you're all expecting, but that's who I am. And I'm going to live true to myself."

What is the first step someone can take toward claiming their onlyness?

Look at what it is you care about. I tell people to do this by asking two questions. First, what is your history and experience that has informed and shaped what you care about? Sometimes when I ask this question, people will say things like, "I really care about equity and people's safety," but they won't share their personal dark side of that story. They won't own it. When you claim your history and experience, both the positive and the negative of it, you tap into the depth of understanding what you care about.

Second, ask, "What would I do with all that?" The way I actually phrase it is, "If you had the magic wand in Disney movies that turns pumpkins into carriages and mice into horses, what would you use the wand to do?" Usually as soon as I ask that question, people have something that sparks in their mind.

Then I say, "OK, now combine those two things for a minute—your history, experience, visions, and hopes, plus that magic wand moment of what you wish you could change. Where does that lead you?" Usually that process can really clarify what you care about, and then you have a better idea of how your onlyness can be powerful.

I also want to ask about fitting in, because there's no one I've ever met who doesn't relate to the concept of, "Oh, my gosh, do I fit in?" What's the relationship between that worry and anxiety?

Research has found that 61% of people say they cover up their true selves at work. Well over a majority of people in a room are trying to fake it. Even 45% of white men say they do it.

We're all dying to be ourselves. That's the big lesson. We give so much permission to certain people in the organization to be themselves, and then the rest of us try to figure out how to fit in. What we need is a range of leadership constructs, a range of ways of being able to show up to work with all of our different perspectives. That's how we'll shape the workplace so that it's more human.

Morra Aarons-Mele is an entrepreneur, online marketing expert, and communications executive who founded the award-winning strategic communications agency Women Online and The Mission List, an influencer database. She helped Hillary Clinton log on for her first internet chat, and has launched digital campaigns for former President Obama, Malala Yousafzai, the United Nations, and many other leading figures and organizations. An extremely anxious introvert herself, Morra hosts top-rated podcast *The Anxious Achiever* for HBR Presents from *Harvard Business Review*. She's passionate about helping people rethink the relationship between their mental health and their leadership.

Angela Neal-Barnett is a professor of psychological sciences and the director of the program for research on anxiety disorders among African Americans at Kent

State University. The first Black woman to be promoted to full professor in the College of Arts and Sciences, she is the author of *Soothe Your Nerves: The Black Woman's Guide to Understanding and Overcoming Anxiety, Panic, and Fear*. Every day, she takes time to protect her spirit and her mental health. Follow her on Twitter @dranjela.

Nilofer Merchant is a former Apple executive, an author of three notable books on innovation, and was ranked as one of the top management leaders of our time four times in a row by Thinkers50.

CHAPTER 8

Supporting Women's Mental Health

by Kelly Greenwood

While men and women have similar rates of mental health conditions overall, women face specific challenges around mental health in the workplace. Some are tied to gender roles and stereotypes, and some are intersectional in nature. In fact, mental health is intersectional, since identity markers such as race and gender shape an individual's experience; it's also an emerging diversity, equity, and inclusion (DEI) category in and of itself.

The list of challenges affecting women is long. For one, women are more prone to certain diagnoses. They

Adapted from "How Organizations Can Support Women's Mental Health at Work," on hbr.org, March 18, 2022 (product #H06X31).

are twice as likely as men to experience depression, generalized anxiety disorder, and PTSD, and much more likely to battle eating disorders.[1] Pay inequity, caregiving responsibilities, and gender-based violence are among the contributing risk factors to common mental health conditions.[2] Infertility, menopause, and postpartum depression also affect many.

Physical and emotional caregiving roles—as daughters, mothers, colleagues, and even leaders—result in heavier burdens. Then there's being underrepresented in leadership at work, navigating "double only" status as a woman of color or member of the LGBTQ+ community, enduring sexual harassment, dealing with imposter syndrome, juggling parental leave, and having office housekeeping roles. Many of these challenges are largely invisible, since women may be reluctant to discuss them at all, much less at work.

Add these up, and it's no surprise that gender brings another layer of complexity to workplace mental health. The structures and systems of most companies were built with men in mind. Many women may not be inclined to "other" themselves further by disclosing a mental health challenge.

Between my gender and generalized anxiety disorder, I've had a lot to navigate, and I've done my fair share of covering. This has been the case in environments ranging from male-dominated management consulting at the start of my career to my current role as founder and CEO of Mind Share Partners, a nonprofit driving culture change on workplace mental health.

Here's what to do if you're a woman struggling with your mental health at work, or if you're a leader who wants to create a mentally healthy environment for your female employees. Many of these recommendations are standard to supporting mental health at work, but the nuances and context of being a woman make applying them much more difficult.

How Women Can Advocate for Their Own Mental Health at Work

Despite the systemic issues at play, there are practical ways that you can advocate for your mental health in the workplace. These include identifying and asking for what you need, finding allies and safe spaces, talking to your manager or HR, and evaluating your culture to decide whether it supports you in the ways you want.

Reflect on your needs

First, think through the nature of your mental health and your specific challenge. Is it chronic, episodic, or a one-time event? Consider the contributing factors. Are they work related or limited to your personal life? Is there a gender-specific component, like childcare or workplace discrimination, that might make you more reluctant to discuss the problem at work? Be clear about the effects. Is your mental health challenge affecting your work performance?

Talk with a friend, family member, or therapist about your concerns and brainstorm the potential requests that you could make at work to support yourself. You may also want to get advice from a women's circle or ask female friends to recommend therapists, books, or podcasts that focus on gender. Consider whether seeking out the mental health benefits and other resources your employer provides (such as health-care coverage to see a therapist or psychiatrist) is sufficient or if you need an accommodation (such as starting your workday later). It may help to educate yourself about the legal protections available to you. (See chapter 1 for more.)

Find allies and safe spaces

The first person I ever disclosed my generalized anxiety disorder to at work was a female mentor who had previously told me about a family member's mental health struggles. Without this knowledge, I wouldn't have had the courage to seek her guidance when I was underperforming as a direct result of my anxiety.

Given the stigma often associated with mental health challenges, finding a safe space to tell your story and receive support from allies is a critical step. Simply realizing that you're not alone can go a long way, especially when you may be feeling othered because of your gender. This can happen one-on-one or through the women's affinity group or mental health employee resource group at your company. Peer support is a powerful lever to reduce stigma.

Allies can help you see that mental health challenges can be useful for developing workplace strengths. Combined with the added difficulty of navigating gender at work, allies can teach us empathy and resilience, spur creativity, and fuel our ambition, as has been the case for me.

If there aren't any obvious mental health allies at your company (of any gender), look for potential indicators. Has someone expressed vulnerability or talked authentically about personal challenges of any kind? Has a male leader referenced his working wife or daughter in a supportive way? Test the waters to see how they respond to, say, a celebrity who's been in the news for talking about her mental health or an upcoming fundraising walk in your community to support a mental health organization. Then consider seeking advice on how to navigate your specific workplace.

Talk to your manager or HR

If you need accommodations for your mental health or have suggestions that could benefit everyone, talk with your manager (or HR if you don't feel comfortable with your manager). This can be scary. Mind Share Partners' *Mental Health at Work 2021 Report* found that women respondents were less comfortable talking about their mental health with managers and HR than men were, but no difference existed when talking to colleagues or friends.[3] Power dynamics are at play, sometimes made more pronounced by gender. You may fear putting an already hard-to-come-by promotion in jeopardy or othering yourself with a mental health challenge or stereotypically "female" concern such as childcare or eldercare.

You control how much you choose to share and with whom. Your request can be as simple as, "Could I take

Friday off? I've been feeling a little burned out lately." You might mention your diagnosis if you have a close, trusting relationship. If your proposed solution involves changes to workplace factors that could benefit everyone on your team, such as increased flexibility or norms around after-hours response times, you might introduce the idea of a working-styles conversation with your manager. This sets up everyone to do their best work and supports mental health without having to name it. Should you require a separate accommodation, you'll likely have to partner with your manager and HR to cocreate a solution. (See chapter 1 for more.)

Even in a female-led workplace, my self-stigma and fear of professional repercussions were so strong that, as a new hire trying to prove myself, I didn't ask for the simple accommodation to see my therapist in person weekly. Had I done that early on, I would have saved my manager, my organization, and myself a lot of hardship. Reflect on the trade-offs of sharing; they may increasingly be weighted toward disclosure as mental health challenges become more normalized, especially among high performers.

Evaluate the culture

While quitting is a last resort when your job is hurting your mental health, it should always be on the table. Before you make that decision, take a step back and consider your company's culture. Are there women in leadership? Anyone who has openly talked about their mental health or other challenges? Is the executive team open to feedback and change? Is it committed to DEI and new ways of working that promote balance and well-being?

You shouldn't have to jeopardize your mental health to earn a living. Fortunately, companies are realizing that more and more as employee priorities around mental health play out through recruitment and retention. It's OK to walk away from work that isn't working. The *Mental Health at Work 2021 Report* found that 68% of millennials and 81% of Gen Zers have left jobs for mental health reasons, compared with 50% of respondents overall. The report also found that women were less likely than men to positively view their organization's culture around mental health. A study from Deloitte showed that women who work for gender-inclusive organizations have higher levels of mental well-being and loyalty to their employers.[4] To compete for talent, companies will have to make changes, as younger generations are increasingly prioritizing their mental health and working in cultures that support it.

How Leaders Can Support Women's Mental Health

Unless we're in positions of power, there is only so much that individual women can do to advocate for their mental health. Leaders, managers, and HR must drive culture change to correct for historically male-dominated workplaces. To do just that, we offer the following advice, much of it adapted with women in mind from the Mind Share Partners' Ecosystem of a Mentally Healthy Workplace framework.[5]

Be the change

Lead through your actions to model what would have helped the younger you, regardless of your gender. Authentic leadership is an extremely effective, evidence-based way to gain trust and lessen stigma. Being vulnerable and sharing about your own mental health or other challenges is one of the most powerful things you can do. It signals to employees that they can discuss what was once taboo in the workplace and helps them to feel comfortable sharing.

I now freely talk about my past mental health challenges and push myself to share my current struggles in real time to benefit my team. These range from debilitating depression that led to a leave of absence, to grief about my dad's unexpected passing immediately before the Covid-19 pandemic, to hot flashes due to perimenopause, which felt particularly off limits, given my early days in male-dominated consulting. Revealing that last one ended up being an unexpected win since my team gifted me a mini desk fan that plugs into my laptop! Members of my team have told me how refreshing it is to see a female leader be vulnerable. As a result of my sharing, they can freely discuss their own mental health and personal challenges for the first time ever at work, allowing us to offer support and adjust as needed.

Modeling mentally healthy behaviors and building a culture of connection are also essential, especially for women, who may be hesitant to disrupt the status quo. Just telling people that it's OK to take a vacation or log off after working hours does nothing if you don't follow that same advice. For example, I put my therapy appointments and events for my kids' school on my work calendar. My team knows that they can also prioritize important personal things during the workday and that kids can pop into our video meetings. Checking in regularly on a personal level with each of your direct reports fosters a caring and inclusive culture. This can be as simple as reserving the first five minutes of a meeting to genuinely ask, "How are you, and how can I help?"

Provide mental health training and overcommunicate resources

Leaders must prioritize mental health training for people at all levels, including executive teams, managers, and individual contributors. Due to generational and other differences in the workplace, everyone should have the same level of understanding, including how mental health intersects with the various aspects of our identities—gender and otherwise.

Take a proactive, preventive approach with a management lens. It isn't necessary to dive into signs and symptoms. Mental health training should provide baseline knowledge, discuss intersectionality, dispel myths, and offer tools and strategies to navigate workplace mental health, such as how to have difficult conversations and create mentally healthy cultures.

In addition, leaders should regularly communicate about the mental health benefits available. These should be embedded in companywide emails at least monthly and be prominently featured on the intranet, instead of buried deep within a benefits portal. Since many people delay seeking treatment due to stigma, leaders should share if they have personally used the benefits, to normalize doing so. This should also be true of other benefits that women may not want to discuss openly, such as those for infertility.

Build mental health into policies, practices, and measurement

Name mental health explicitly in relevant policies and incorporate it into organizationwide practices. Examples include paid time off and leaves as well as flexible hours and healthy communication norms. Companies should establish a genuine commitment to DEI, including having executive sponsors and funding for employee resource groups. (See chapter 20 for more on ERGs.)

In addition, leaders must rectify structural issues that harm women, such as pay inequity, insufficient parental leaves, and lack of consequences for microaggressions and harassment.

Leaders can incite positive changes through accountability mechanisms such as regular surveys. Measuring female employee engagement, retention, and dimensions of mental health cements the support of women's mental health as an organizational priority.

Foster inclusive flexibility and sustainable ways of working

Workplace factors such as lack of autonomy, unrealistic workloads, and lack of boundaries after hours can lead to poor mental health. For women, these can be even more detrimental due to microaggressions, caregiving responsibilities, and other factors. I often avoid mentioning my two small children to external male stakeholders for fear of biases about my capacity to simultaneously be a mother and an entrepreneur.

Leaders should build as much flexibility as possible into policies and practices. Everyone will need something different, be it remote work or flexible hours. Be sure to revisit this with your direct reports, since shifts happen over time and with life changes such as parenthood.

Additionally, leaders should model sustainable and flexible work practices themselves. Otherwise, female employees are unlikely to change their behavior, fearing negative implications for their career. Even in the most supportive environments, we typically have to unlearn a lifetime of conditioning—whether around workaholism or mental health stigma. Many women learn to put their own needs last, to be people pleasers rather than to speak up for ourselves, and to do the extra emotional labor required to balance being strong yet nurturing leaders. This can make prioritizing mental health at work exceedingly difficult. We should give ourselves grace and remember that we can only be effective once we've first taken care of ourselves, including our mental health.

Reorienting to support women's mental health at work will ultimately benefit everyone, from dads who want to be more involved parents to Gen Zers who expect flexibility by default. Hopefully there will come a time when we won't have to separate out the needs of women, but instead will have achieved true culture change and inclusion.

———————

Kelly Greenwood is the founder and CEO of Mind Share Partners, a nonprofit that is changing the culture of workplace mental health so that both employees and organizations can thrive. It provides training and strategic advising to leading companies, hosts communities to support ERGs and professionals, and builds public awareness. Kelly has learned to manage her generalized anxiety disorder, which has twice led to debilitating depression. She founded Mind Share Partners to create the resources that she wished she, her managers, and her organization had had when she was struggling. Follow her on Twitter @KellyAGreenwood.

NOTES

1. "Diversity and Health Equity Education, Women," American Psychiatric Association, https://www.psychiatry.org/psychiatrists/cultural-competency/education/women-patients.

2. "Diversity and Health Equity Education, Women," American Psychiatric Association.

3. Mind Share Partners, *Mental Health at Work 2021 Report*, https://www.mindsharepartners.org/mentalhealthatworkreport-2021.

4. "Women @ Work: A Global Outlook," Deloitte, n.d., https://www2.deloitte.com/global/en/pages/about-deloitte/articles/women-at-work-global-outlook.html.

5. "Creating Mentally Healthy Workplaces and Programs," Mind Share Partners, n.d., https://www.mindsharepartners.org/workplacementalhealthframework.

CHAPTER 9

Prioritizing the Mental Health of People of Color

by Angela Neal-Barnett

Too often, we mistakenly assume that mental health is the same for everyone, and that race and ethnicity are not factors. But disparities exist between people of color and their white counterparts in the prevalence, incidence, symptoms, and treatment of mental health conditions. The Covid-19 pandemic and the wider recognition of racism as a public health crisis have highlighted these disparities, along with the need to acknowledge and address them in the workplace.

The Barriers You Face

If you're a person of color, barriers to mental health assistance include the impact of racism, being an "only," cultural mistrust, and collectivism. Understanding racism and its impact is key to advocating for your mental health in the workplace and for raising the awareness of leaders.

Racism takes three forms, each of which is a chronic stressor. *Systemic racism* is when ideologies, institutions, and policies operate to produce racial and ethnic inequality (such as your firm only hiring "qualified" people of color, or employees of color only being assigned clients of color). *Interpersonal racism* involves two or more people and can be manifested through bigotry, bias, prejudice, and microaggressions (such as a colleague making an offensive comment to you). *Internalized racism* is the acceptance of negative stereotypes and societal beliefs about your racial group (such as believing you were only hired because of your race or ethnicity).

Research shows that experiencing or observing racism impacts someone on a cellular level, aging them at a faster rate and placing them at higher risk for mental health concerns.[1] If you're a person of color, you likely experience one or more forms of racism on a daily basis. As a result, you are at higher risk for anxiety and depression as well as stress and trauma disorders. For some disorders (anxiety and trauma), the symptoms experienced by Black Americans are more intense and last longer.

Employees of color tend to be an only—the only person of their race in the department, the division, and in some cases the entire office. When you're an only, you can go days, weeks, even months without seeing or speaking to coworkers who look like you. This means you have no one to check in with about whether their race-related office experiences are similar to yours. ("Does that boss check everyone's work, or just mine?") Being an only also means that if you are not at a meeting or don't attend an outing, people notice and comment. This can create or add to a sense of anxiety and isolation in the workplace.

Onlyness and racism in their various forms lead to another barrier to receiving care—cultural mistrust, the tendency not to believe or trust your white colleagues or leaders. This mistrust has several effects: You are wary and keep your guard up, leading your colleagues to see you as unfriendly or not a team player. When it comes to your mental health, cultural mistrust heightens concerns that any request you make for care or accommodations will be used to deny you promotions and raises, or may result in the loss of your job. Worse yet, you may believe your request will be shared with the entire office. Simply stated, you believe you will be betrayed, and this belief in turn fuels mistrust.

Many employees of color are raised in families and communities that embrace collectivism, the belief that your successes and failures are not yours alone but are shared by your family and community. When difficulties arise, you may feel as though you have let the family or community down. You are unable to recognize that at some point everybody faces mental health challenges. You feel ashamed, embarrassed, and unworthy of help or forgiveness. So you do not ask for help and you do not respond to those who offer it. As a result, the impact of whatever you are struggling with—depression, anxiety, trauma—increases.

Assessing the State of Your Mental Health

Mental health is rarely discussed in communities of color; the common perception is that it is a "white" problem and that poor mental health equals "crazy." Nothing could be further from the truth. In my corporate mental health workshops for people of color, when I explain in detail the signs and symptoms of depression, anxiety, or trauma, the common response from people of color is, "This has a name? I thought it was the way I was supposed to feel." That's usually followed by the question, "How do I know if I need help?"

The following questions are a good way to assess your mental health:

- Is the way I am feeling or the thoughts I am experiencing interfering in my life?

- Is the way I am feeling or the thoughts I am experiencing preventing me from doing the things I want to do?

- Is the way I am feeling or the thoughts I am experiencing making it difficult for me to be present in any or all aspects of my life?

If the answer to any of these questions is yes, it is time to pay closer attention to your mental well-being and ask for support and help.

Asking for help is not always easy. The interaction between racism, cultural mistrust, and onlyness can make it feel like a sign of weakness, like mental health is a problem you cannot solve on your own. When you feel this way, remind yourself that mental health is health—if you had a problem with your body, you wouldn't hesitate to get help. Your mental health should be no different, and not seeking help when you need it allows the sense of shame and weakness to fester.

The first step in asking for help is identifying the best person to ask. Is there a manager (perhaps your own) or other leader in the company who you believe will listen? Often, a company has identified someone in HR to assist employees with mental health concerns. When you ask for help, be specific. Do you want a therapist, a group, a class? Whatever you believe will work best for you, ask for it. It's OK if you don't know what to ask for or what type of intervention you want. You can simply say, "I've noticed that I've been more anxious (or stressed, angry, depressed) lately at work and would like help for this. What options are available? What have others found useful?"

Despite efforts to address the barriers, some workplaces remain detrimental to your mental health as a person of color. In these situations, you must determine if it's in your best interest to leave. Making this decision with a therapist can help reduce the anxiety and fear that may arise. A therapist will help you evaluate the pros and cons of leaving, develop an exit strategy, and think through steps to take for your future, including what to look for in your next company.

If you do leave, the company may require you to participate in an exit interview. When asked about your reasons for leaving, try as best as you can to remain unemotional (as difficult as that may be) and stick to the facts. Sadly, and unfairly, it is easier for the interviewer to dismiss your experiences or suggestions if you are seen as overly emotional.

What Managers and Companies Can Do

In recent years I have spent a significant amount of time consulting in corporations and companies on the mental health of employees of color. Initially, I am invited in because the situation has reached a crisis level—for example, an employee of color has had an outburst, or employees of color have demanded that the company address their mental health needs. As a leader, you can't wait until the mental health of your employees of color is in crisis mode to make it a priority. Research shows that prioritizing the mental health of employees of color from the outset enhances the workplace environment, promotes wellness, improves productivity, and increases profits.[2]

As a leader, you must emphasize by thought, word, and deed that there is no weakness, shame, retribution, or judgment when an employee of color (or any employee) asks for assistance. This can be accomplished by incorporating a segment on mental health and wellness into staff meetings, being sure to address the needs of employees of color. And mental health first-aid training can become part of supervisors' training, providing those in leadership with the skills to respond empathetically and appropriately to employees of color who seek help.

Systemic and interpersonal racism in the workplace puts employees of color at higher risk for mental health challenges. Leaders must be willing to take a hard look at policies and procedures that reflect systemic racism and workplace cultures that may be rife with interpersonal racism. Then, they must work to rethink and change those policies, procedures, and cultures.

Empowering employees of color to protect and prioritize their mental health involves ensuring that therapists of color and culturally competent therapists and counselors are available through the employee assistance program (EAP) or company insurance plan. Most employees of color want a therapist who looks like them. However, currently the number of therapists of color is unfortunately small. Thus, the inclusion of culturally competent therapists *who have previous experience* counseling employees of color is critical. Due to cultural mistrust, some employees of color will request a therapist outside the EAP and indicate their willingness to forgo the insurance plan and self-pay. In these cases, HR should compile and make available a list of therapists of color and white therapists.

As employees of color prioritize their mental health, they may require certain accommodations. Mental health accommodations are part of the Americans with Disabilities Act, which employers should familiarize themselves with. In addition, information about an employee's mental health is health information and by law remains confidential. Common accommodations include breaks, a limit on hours worked, and the use of a service animal. Because mental health and faith are deeply entwined for many people of color, requests for accommodations may include things such as extending the lunch hour to attend midday prayer services or playing faith-based music in their workspace.

Leaders should keep in mind that the barriers to asking for help, described earlier, make people of color feel vulnerable when they seek accommodations. Managers should be familiar with and understand these obstacles and look for signs that they are interfering with a request for accommodations. An example of this might be someone who is an only becoming more isolated at work.

HR and DEI directors who are witnessing resignations among employees of color should face the problem calmly, openly, and honestly. Investigate the factors behind the company's failure to protect their mental health. Climate surveys, exit interviews, and focus groups are insufficient. Rather, you must observe and understand the daily work experiences of employees of color. (One simple example: Was a departing employee of color an only in their department or division?) Once you identify the root causes, create and implement an action plan with clear steps and deadlines. And do not be afraid to bring in outside help—the expertise and knowledge to address the problem areas may not exist in-house.

If you're a person of color, these steps can help you deal with the mental health struggles you're facing at work, even deciding whether your company is a place you can thrive. If you're a leader, make it a priority to find out more about how your employees of color really feel at work and how you can support them. Doing so is a win for the employees and the business alike.

––––––––––––

Angela Neal-Barnett, PhD, is a professor of psychological sciences and the director of the program for research on anxiety disorders among African Americans at Kent State University. The first Black woman to be promoted to full professor in the College of Arts and Sciences, she is the author of *Soothe Your Nerves: The Black Woman's Guide to Understanding and Overcoming Anxiety, Panic, and Fear.* Every day, she takes time to protect her spirit and her mental health. Follow her on Twitter @dranjela.

NOTES

1. Sierra E. Carter et al., "The Effect of Early Discrimination on Accelerated Aging Among African Americans," *Health Psychology* 38, no. 11 (2019): 1010–1013.

2. Lene E. Søvold et al., "Prioritizing the Mental Health and Well-Being of Healthcare Workers: An Urgent Global Public Priority," *Frontiers in Public Health*, May 7, 2021, https://www.frontiersin.org/articles/10.3389/fpubh.2021.679397/full.

Supporting Mental Health as a Manager

CHAPTER 10

Reduce the Stigma of Mental Health at Work

by Diana O'Brien and Jen Fisher

At work, those suffering from a mental health issue—either a clinical condition or something less severe—often hide it for fear that they may face discrimination from peers or even bosses. These stigmas can and must be overcome. But it takes more than policies set at the top. It also requires empathetic action from managers on the ground.

We count ourselves among those who have wrestled with mental health challenges. One morning a few years ago, in the midst of a successful year, Jen couldn't get out

Adapted from "5 Ways Bosses Can Reduce the Stigma of Mental Health at Work," on hbr.org, February 19, 2019 (product #H04SVU).

of bed. As a driven professional, she had ignored all the warning signs that she was experiencing post-traumatic stress disorder (PTSD). But her mentor, Diana, could see something was wrong, and when Jen couldn't come to work, the gravity of the situation became even clearer. In the ensuing weeks, we worked together to get Jen the help she needed.

Diana understood Jen's struggles because she had been there, too—not with PTSD but with anxiety. As the mother of adult triplets with autism and a busy job, she'd often had difficulty managing things in her own life.

Throughout both of our careers, we have moved across the spectrum of mental health from thriving to barely hanging on, and somewhere in between. What we've learned through our own experiences is how much managerial support matters.

When bosses understand mental health issues—and how to respond to them—it can make all the difference for an employee professionally and personally. This involves taking notice, offering a helping hand, and saying, "I'm here, I have your back, you are not alone."

That's exactly what Jen said when a coworker told her that he was grappling with anxiety; it had gotten to the point where it was starting to impact his work and his relationships at home. He came to her because she'd been open about her own struggles. She listened to him, worked to understand what accommodations he needed, and told him about available resources, such as employee assistance programs. Then she continued to check in to see he was getting the support he needed and make it clear that she and others were there to help.

How do you learn or teach the people on your team to address colleagues' or direct reports' mental health issues in the same way? Here are five ways managers can help drive a more empathetic culture.

Pay attention to language

We all need to be aware of the words we use that can contribute to stigmatizing mental health issues: "Mr. OCD is at it again—organizing everything." "She's totally schizo today!" "He is being so bipolar this week—one minute he's up, the next he's down." We've heard comments like these, maybe even made them ourselves. But through the ears of a colleague who has a mental health challenge, they can sound like indictments. Would you open up about a disorder or tell your team leader you needed time to see a therapist after hearing these words?

Rethink "sick days"

If you have cancer, no one says, "Let's just push through" or "Can you learn to deal with it?" They recognize that it's an illness and you'll need to take time off to treat it. If you have the flu, your manager will tell you to go home and rest. But few people in business would react to emotional outbursts or other signs of stress, anxiety, or manic behavior in the same way. We need to get more comfortable with the idea of suggesting and requesting days to focus on improving mental as well as physical health.

Encourage open and honest conversations

It's important to create safe spaces for people to talk about their own challenges, past and present, without fear of being called "unstable" or passed up for the next big project or promotion. Employees shouldn't fear that they will be judged or excluded if they open up in this way. Leaders can set the tone for this by sharing their own experiences, as we've done, or stories of other people who have struggled with mental health issues, gotten help, and resumed successful careers. They should also explicitly encourage everyone to speak up when feeling overwhelmed or in need.

Be proactive

Not all stress is bad, and people in high-pressure careers often grow accustomed to it or develop coping mechanisms. However, prolonged unmanageable stress can contribute to worsening symptoms of mental illness. How can managers ensure their employees are finding the right balance? By offering access to programs, resources, and education on stress management and resilience-building. In our marketplace survey on employee burnout, nearly 70% of respondents said that their employers were not doing enough to prevent or alleviate burnout. Bosses need to do a better job of helping their employees connect to resources before stress leads to more serious problems.

Train people to notice and respond

Most offices keep a medical kit around in case someone needs a bandage or an aspirin. We've also begun to train our people in Mental Health First Aid, a national program proven to increase people's ability to recognize the signs of someone who may be struggling with a mental health challenge and connect them to support resources. Through role-plays and other activities, they offer guidance in how to listen nonjudgmentally, offer reassurance, and assess the risk of suicide or self-harm when, for example, a colleague is suffering a panic attack or reacting to a traumatic event. These can be difficult, emotionally charged conversations, and they can come at unexpected times, so it's important to be ready for them.

When your people are struggling, you want them to be able to open up and ask for help. These five strategies can help any boss or organization create a culture that ceases to stigmatize mental illness.

Diana O'Brien retired from her role as global chief marketing officer of Deloitte and is currently a board member and business adviser.

Jen Fisher is Deloitte's chief well-being officer in the United States and a leading voice on workplace well-being and the importance of mental health and social connection in our personal and professional lives. She's also the coauthor of the bestselling book *Work Better Together* and the host of the podcast *WorkWell*. Jen is open about her own struggles with overcoming burnout and dealing with anxiety to help reduce mental health stigmas in the workplace.

CHAPTER 11

When Your Employee Discloses a Mental Health Condition

by Amy Gallo

When one of your direct reports has the courage to talk with you about their mental health condition, how you respond is critical. You want the person to know you appreciate them sharing, while also reassuring them that their job and your perception of them are not at risk. At the same time, you need to figure out what impact, if any, this will have on your team and their workload. What do

---

Adapted from content posted on hbr.org, February 23, 2021 (product #H067KD).

you say right away? What questions do you ask? How do you decide what accommodations, if any, to make?

What the Experts Say

It's important to keep in mind that the employee likely had to overcome a lot of fear to talk with you about this topic. "The person has done something difficult and risky by raising this issue. In most cases, a tremendous amount of thought has gone into the decision," says Kelly Greenwood, founder and CEO of Mind Share Partners, a nonprofit that focuses on changing the culture of workplace mental health. "The disclosure decision is complex," says Susan Goldberg, core doctoral faculty member at Fielding Graduate University, and it depends on the "individual's personal situation, the particular employer, and societal issues." Therefore, it's important to handle these interactions the right way. The good news is that these can be productive conversations, as long as you follow a few pieces of advice.

Thank them for telling you

Start off by acknowledging the effort it took for the employee to tell you. "If nothing else happens in the first conversation, be sure to thank the person for sharing," says Greenwood. But don't make it a big deal. Your goal should be to normalize the topic as much as possible. She says that even if this is the first time you're having a conversation like this, they happen all the time. "Your reaction shouldn't convey, 'This is a big serious issue,' because that could increase their shame or fear about their future," she says. Goldberg also cautions against being overly emotional. "You don't want the employee to have to deal with your reaction." Your response should be consistent with your relationship. "This is not the time to act like a friend if you don't have a close, trusting relationship. Nor should you be distant if you've been close up to this point," she says. In other words, treat the person and this conversation the same way you have in the past.

Listen

Give the person space to say what they want to say and tell you what they need in terms of flexibility or accommodations. "Listen actively with an open mind and without judgment," says Greenwood. Pay attention to your nonverbal cues. "If you're acting skittish or uncomfortable, it's discouraging for your employee because it sends a message that you don't want to talk about it," says Greenwood. You can adopt a curious mindset, but hold back from asking a ton of questions, especially ones that require that the person disclose more information than you need. For example, "you don't need to know what the disability they have is called," says Goldberg, or how long they've had it. Let them lead the way in how much they want to tell you.

Tell them you want to support them— but don't overpromise

It can be tempting to tell the person (especially if they're a high performer) that you'll do whatever it takes to support them, but you want to tread carefully.

It may be that they're just telling you as an FYI, says Goldberg, and they don't need you to make any adjustments to their workload or schedule. Don't make assumptions. If they're asking for time off or changes to their work schedule, be careful not to overpromise. Instead, make clear that your intention is to partner with them to sort it out. For example, you might say, "I hope I've made it clear that you are a valuable member of this team and organization. We'll figure this out together." In this initial conversation, you don't have to have all the answers readily available. Give yourself permission to not have the perfect response and to figure out what's possible. Greenwood suggests you say, "Thank you so much for sharing. Let me take some time to digest and get back to you on X day." Be specific about when you'll have the next conversation so they don't have to worry.

Don't make it about you

It's possible that you or someone you're close with has been through something similar, but don't focus the conversation on you. Keep in mind that "everyone is different in terms of how their condition shows up. My anxiety is different from another person's anxiety," says Greenwood, and "you can't assume you understand what they're going through or the extent to which it's affecting their work." That said, sometimes sharing a personal story can help to normalize the topic. If you have the kind of relationship with the employee where you share personal stories, just be sure that what you share is hopeful. Don't talk about someone who never got better or had to quit their job, and don't downplay their experience by insisting everything will be OK because it was for you or someone else.

Maintain confidentiality

Tell the employee that you will make every effort to honor confidentiality but that you may need to speak with HR. If the person is uncomfortable with that, or worried about having something go into their employment file, you might say, "I may have to tell them eventually, but I can talk in generalities, without naming you, at first." It can be helpful, says Greenwood, to explain to the employee why you may have to tell HR. This includes ensuring that the employee gets the legal protections they're entitled to in order to avoid discrimination as well as access to all the company's resources and possible accommodations. She also notes that, depending on where you live, a manager may be required by law to go to HR once someone has disclosed a mental health condition, even if the employee hasn't requested an accommodation. If you're unsure about local regulations, feel free to first talk to HR without using the employee's name.

But, as much as possible, keep the information to yourself. "It's tempting to talk to others about it for your own emotional support—or to explain why you're moving work around—but it's not OK unless the employee expressly gives you permission to disclose," says Greenwood. In some cases, the employee may give you permission or even ask you to let others know. If they do, make sure that you are clear in any communication that the person has asked you to tell others, so no one thinks you're talking behind the employee's back.

Consider what changes you can make

There is a variety of things that your employee may want or need so that they can take care of their mental health. These might include keeping different hours, working alone or in a group, taking time off to see a doctor, or having occasional "mental health days." Whether or not you can grant these requests will often depend on your company's existing policies. Greenwood says it's important for managers to know the difference between accommodations, which are formal, reactive exceptions to existing policies for a specific employee after a disclosure, and adaptations, which are proactive adjustments you can make for everyone that are within the company's policies, such as flexible hours. If you need to make accommodations for an employee, it's critical to involve HR (more on that later), who will be familiar with the national and local laws that determine what you're legally allowed to do.

Some of the changes made to working hours or workload might impact other people on your team, and you'll have to figure out "what to tell employees who ask why this person is coming in late, or experiencing different treatment," says Goldberg. She suggests that you keep your answers to any questions straightforward and simple. For example, you might say, "It's an accommodation," or "We worked out different hours." Talk with the employee about how they would prefer you address any concerns that come up from their colleagues.

Ask for help from others

This person came to you because you're their manager. "It's not your role to be their therapist, doctor, or lawyer," says Greenwood. Don't offer health or legal advice. And don't try to figure this out on your own. Whenever possible, work with HR to come up with possible solutions—and let the employee know that's what you will do. "The ideal situation, if an accommodation is required, is that you cocreate a solution for the person with HR and the employee," she says. "Hopefully HR can provide you with a 'menu of options' of what they've provided in the past." You don't want to put it on the employee to come up with those options, unless they'd like to. Greenwood says that when she disclosed her anxiety to a previous boss, she "was not in a place to be thinking out of the box."

In small companies, or those without a supportive HR department, it may be up to you to figure out what you can do. Goldberg's research shows that smaller companies often have the ability to offer more flexibility, but "it can also be more challenging because you may not be able to afford what they're asking for."[1]

Refer them to other resources, if available

There may be other resources inside your company that you can refer them to. "We're seeing more and more employee resource groups form around issues of mental health, often started by more junior employees," says Greenwood. You can point the person to those groups, if available. (See chapter 20 for more.) You can also direct them to any mental health benefits that your company offers, such as therapy or meditation apps. If you don't have those resources you can suggest they contact an employee assistance program (EAP), but keep in mind that not all EAPs are high quality, and while one can play an important role in supporting the employee, it's not sufficient on its own. Clinical care is best left to a professional, but you are still responsible, as their manager, for the employee's work experience.

Make yourself "tell-able"

Ideally, we'd all work for a manager whom we felt comfortable talking to when we needed help balancing work with our mental health. Unfortunately, that's not always the case. But you can make it more likely that people will come to you by being a role model. Greenwood emphasizes the importance of leaders and managers talking openly about these issues. "You don't necessarily have to talk about your own mental health condition if you have one, but it could be about your kid having a hard time sleeping, or concerns you have about burning out. You want to show that managers are fallible and human," she says. Being vulnerable in this way gives people a small opening so they in turn feel more comfortable sharing. And, if you hold a powerful position in your organization, sharing your personal experience with mental health, whether it's addressing it directly or, say, openly blocking out your calendar to go to therapy, can go a long way toward normalizing the discussion in your organization and demonstrating that it's possible to succeed at the highest levels when you have a mental health condition.

Case Study: Be Flexible When You Can

Jimmy McMillan, the owner of Heart Life Insurance, suspected that one of his employees, a case manager, was struggling. She was responsible for document processing, customer service, and chasing doctors' offices for records. "She was fantastic most days," Jimmy says, and she'd even work late to finish important documents. But there were other days when "she was nowhere to be found and no one could get in touch with her via phone, text, or email. It was strange; she would just vanish."

When she wasn't available in this way, it meant that the other staff had to work longer hours. Jimmy knew something was going on, but he wasn't sure what. During a regular performance review, he decided to bring it up. "It was a delicate conversation," he says. He was straightforward about what he was observing and asked her questions about her absences, without making assumptions or forcing her to share personal information. "I said something like, 'We care about you and you do a fantastic job; however, sometimes things just seem off. Your attendance is inconsistent, and at times it's impossible to get in touch with you. Is everything going OK?'" She confided in him that she had bipolar 1 disorder and was seeing a psychiatrist. She explained that sometimes changes in her medications would lead to mood swings and there were days where she couldn't function. Hence, the absences.

Jimmy knew very little about the disorder. "I knew enough about mental illness to underwrite a life insurance policy . . . but my experience was all secondhand. I didn't know the first thing about trying to lead or manage [someone with bipolar disorder]." So he did some research. "I read up online as much as I could, and I asked other psychiatrists and counselors about it as we crossed paths professionally."

Because this employee was excellent at her job, he wanted to make it work. "I gave her leeway to take time off with short notice, by just sending me a simple one-line email," he explains. He was able to manage the workflow during her absences. "We used project management software that allowed me to assign her tasks to another case manager. When she was ready to work again, we could just assign the tasks back to her and move on."

He said that her disclosure made it much easier to handle her absences. And looking back over the time she was at the company, she didn't take any more time off than anyone else on the team. And "she would always make the time up even though I never asked her to," Jimmy says.

She eventually left the company to work in a local law firm where she could earn a higher salary. Jimmy was sad to see her go, but as he says, "I'd hire her again in a heartbeat." And, he says, he learned a valuable lesson from the experience: "Mental illness should be treated with the same compassion and grace that we give any other serious disease."

Amy Gallo is a contributing editor at *Harvard Business Review* and the author of the *HBR Guide to Dealing with Conflict at Work* and *Getting Along: How to Work with Anyone (Even Difficult People)*. Her years of therapy have informed her thinking on interpersonal dynamics between coworkers and helped her better navigate the stress and anxiety of work. Follow her on Twitter @amyegallo.

NOTE

1. S. G. Goldberg, M. B. Killeen, and B. O'Day, "The Disclosure Conundrum: How People with Psychiatric Disabilities Navigate Employment," *Psychology, Public Policy, and Law*, 11, no. 3 (2005): 463–500, https://psycnet.apa.org/doiLanding?doi=10.1037%2F1076-8971.11.3.463.

CHAPTER 12

Asking About Your Team's Mental Health Without Overstepping

by Deborah Grayson Riegel

Talking about mental health at work can feel tricky at best and terrifying at worst. And not talking about it can become a vicious cycle—the less conversations happen, the more the stigma grows. To break this cycle, managers have to address mental health proactively, strategically, and thoughtfully.

Adapted from "Talking About Mental Health with Your Employees—Without Overstepping," on hbr.org, November 3, 2020 (product #H05YOA).

You have a responsibility to your employees to create an open, inclusive, and safe environment that allows them to bring their whole selves to work. Leaders at all levels need to put mental health "on the table"—to talk about it, invite others to talk about it, and work actively to develop resources and plans for their employees. Doing so will increase the likelihood that your colleagues feel happier, more confident, and more productive.

So how do you start talking about a topic that can make even the bravest leader worry about overstepping? Here are three ways.

Talk about health holistically

Chances are that you'd ask a coworker about the back pain they've been experiencing since they started working from home. You'd probably also ask your team member about the tendon they tore on a recent run. You might even share an update about your seasonal allergies or your indigestion. When you're asking about someone's health, make a note to ask about their mental health, too. It can be as simple as, "It sounds like your back pain is getting better. That's good news. And how are you doing overall these days? I know you've been dealing with a lot of stress." (And then stop talking.)

It's helpful if you are willing to share your own struggles, too, because it normalizes the discussion. You might try, "My allergies are keeping me up at night—and so is my anxiety. It's really hard to get a solid night's sleep when I'm worried about [something you're dealing with]. How about you? What's keeping you up at night?" (And then, again, stop talking.) It's important to note that if you haven't had a close connection with a particular employee in the past, your relationship may be low on psychological safety. To start building that up, take small steps. You might say something like, "I know that you and I haven't typically talked about nonwork topics, but for me, work and nonwork feel like they're blurring together these days. How is everything going for you?"

Don't try to fix people

Leaders often succeed by navigating difficult situations and solving complex problems. But people don't like to be "fixed," so don't try. An employee who believes you see them as broken may worry that you don't see them as capable or credible, which can undermine their confidence and competence. Approach your colleagues with the mindset that they are resourceful, able, and may need your support but not necessarily solutions. You want to be a *bridge* to resources, rather than being the resource yourself.

If someone shares that they are struggling, try saying:

- "What would be most helpful to you right now?"

- "What can I take off your plate?"

- "How can I support you without overstepping?"

- "Let's discuss the resources we have available here, and what else you might need."

- "I've been through something similar. And while I don't want to make this about me, I'm open to sharing my experience with you if and when it would be helpful."

Really listen

Financier Bernard Baruch said, "Most of the successful people I've known are the ones who do more listening than talking." That's not enough to just listen; you need to do it well. But that's not always easy—especially when our own preoccupations, distractions, biases, and judgments get in the way.

If you want to create an environment where your employees feel heard, respected, and cared for, here's how:

- Be clear with yourself and your colleague that your intention for listening is to help.

- Suspend judgment (of yourself and the other person) by noticing when an "approving/disapproving" thought enters your mind. Let it pass or actively send it away.

- Focus on your colleague and their experience, being sure to separate their experience from yours.

- Listen for overall themes, such as social isolation or financial concerns, and don't get mired in the details, which can distract you from the big picture of what's going on with them. Since you're there to support them, rather than solve their problems, you don't need to know the specifics.

- Listen with your eyes as well as your ears. Notice changes in facial expressions, which can give you some cues to what the person is actually feeling— which may be different from what they're saying.

- Recognize that when you start thinking to yourself, "What am I supposed to do?" you've stopped listening.

- Let your colleague know if something is interfering with your ability to really listen, whether it's an urgent email, your child demanding your attention, or your own stress—and offer to reschedule your conversation for a time when you can really attend to them.

As World Health Organization ambassador Liya Kebede said, "Helping others isn't a chore, it is one of the greatest gifts there is." Your willingness to open up an honest conversation about mental health with your employees is exactly the kind of gift that so many people want and need from their leaders.

———————

Deborah Grayson Riegel is a keynote speaker, executive coach, and consultant who has taught leadership communication for Wharton Business School, Columbia Business School's Women in Leadership Program, and the Beijing International MBA Program at Peking University. She is coauthor of *Go to Help: 31 Ways to Offer, Ask for, and Accept Help* and *Overcoming Overthinking: 36 Ways to Tame Anxiety for Work, School, and Life*, both written with her daughter Sophie, a mental health advocate. Deborah has obsessive-compulsive disorder, generalized anxiety disorder, and a tic disorder, and is delighted that she has achieved mental well-being in the face of mental illness.

CHAPTER 13

Managing an Employee with Depression

by Kristen Bell DeTienne, Jill M. Hooley, Cristian Larrocha, and Annsheri Reay

Depression is the leading cause of disability worldwide. One in five Americans are affected by mental health issues, with depression being the most common problem.[1] A 2019 report by Blue Cross Blue Shield found that depression diagnoses are rising at a faster rate for Millennials and teens than for any other generation.[2] All told, the disorder is estimated to cost $44 billion a year in lost productivity in the United States alone.[3]

Adapted from "How to Manage an Employee with Depression," on hbr. org, January 15, 2020 (product #H05D03).

Yet despite this enormous and growing toll, many employers take an ad hoc approach to handling depression among employees. Many managers become aware of mental health issues only when they investigate why a team member is performing poorly. A better scenario would be if employees felt empowered to report a mental health problem and ask for a reasonable accommodation so that their managers can intervene to minimize the damage to the organization and help the employees get back on track.

Here is a guide for managers on how to negotiate work arrangements for individuals with depression.

Learn About the Disorder

It would be easy to think that an employee with depression will first speak with HR staff about work accommodations, but it is likely that your team member (or one of their colleagues) will speak with you first.

Because an employee may come to you without warning, you need to prepare ahead of time and learn about depression and its symptoms. These include loss of interest, decreased energy, feelings of low self-esteem or control, disturbed sleep, and poor concentration.

If you understand the symptoms of depression, then you will be able to anticipate work performance issues and the types of accommodations an employee might request.

Allow a Flexible Schedule

For many companies, a normal work schedule implies being in the office from nine to five. However, an employee suffering from depression may come to you and ask to be in the office later in the day. Sleep problems are common in depression and can involve oversleeping as well as difficulties falling or staying asleep. Helping an employee with a work schedule is therefore a reasonable accommodation. Decades of research suggests that flexible work hours actually increase productivity, commitment to the organization, and retention.

However, if you allow flexible hours, research points to two recommendations.[4] First, if needed, set a window of "core hours" or "core days" in which all team members must be at the office. People dealing with depression benefit from structure but often find it difficult to create structure for themselves. You can help by facilitating this in a sensitive and responsive manner. Second, don't let employees with depression stop interacting with you or other team members. Be on the lookout for avoidance on the part of your employee. Withdrawal only exacerbates the sense of isolation that depressed employees already feel.

When left alone, people with depression are more likely to ruminate on the negative effects of depression. This further worsens the situation. If you suspect that this is happening, check in. What is key here is that you reach out in a supportive and nonjudgmental manner. Research suggests that social relationships at work can act as buffers against depression, and that stronger relationships with managers and peers can lower depression.

Simplify Work Scope

Depressed employees may tell you their workload feels too overwhelming or complicated. Depression can affect cognitive function, and cognitive function can also be affected by lack of sleep.

As a manager, you can help by breaking up large projects into smaller tasks. The benefit of giving smaller, more manageable tasks is that it empowers employees to achieve more frequent experiences of success.

Depression is associated with diminished processing of rewards. The more you, as a manager, can do to reinforce success, the better. Repeated victories over time create new and more frequent positive work experiences. This influences the way employees perceive their environment and increases positive expectancies. These "wins" increase employees' confidence that they can accomplish future tasks assigned to them.

Share Deadlines as Needed

Having too many deadlines can be overwhelming to anyone. Furthermore, those suffering from depression often have a low expectancy of their ability to deal with future stressful events.

When sharing deadlines, communicate only as needed. Yes, a project manager needs to see the timeline for the entire project, but for a specialist on your team, especially one with depression, a full timeline may increase stressors and negative emotions.

As a manager, you can help an employee with depression by breaking down large projects into their component parts. By sharing fewer, shorter-term deadlines, you reduce negative emotions by reducing the input of stressors. Shorter-term deadlines allow employees to see large projects as smaller, more manageable tasks, which research shows creates higher levels of work adherence and productivity. As noted earlier, this approach can also facilitate a sense of agency—something that is frequently compromised in the context of depression.

Focus on Positive Outcomes and Criticize Less

People who are depressed can be highly self-critical. Rather than highlighting failures, focus on supporting and celebrating moments of achievement, such as when employees meet deadlines. Moreover, research shows that people who are criticized by someone whom they perceive as highly critical of them are less able to activate neurocircuits that control negative emotions.

Motivation in depressed employees plummets in the face of threats and punishment. Research suggests that explaining the positive necessity of assignments as a motivation tool is far more effective than sharing the detrimental costs of an unfinished project. Framing assignments in terms of benefits and importance increases their perceived appeal and strengthens intrinsic motivation in employees.

If your employee continues to drop the ball, you may be tempted either to assign them to menial tasks or to penalize them with exceptionally difficult tasks that force the employee to work harder. In reality, it's possible that the person feels as though either one of these scenarios has already occurred. Make sure you assign tasks in a manner that considers someone's current level of functioning—which will change over time as their depression does. Because of this, flexibility on the part of the manager is crucial. Check in with your employees regularly and make sure their work assignments match their current abilities.

Additionally, know the strengths of your employees and play to those strengths. If your employees feel like tasks are designed for them, they'll be more likely to view the tasks as important, complete them quickly, and experience a sense of validation.

This method could be both immediately and ultimately beneficial, as research shows that people who feel as though assignments are useful and tailored specifically to their abilities are more interested in the assignments and experience diminished levels of depression in the long term.[5]

Be a Leader

Coping with depression is difficult, not only for the person with depression but also for those with whom the depressed person interacts. So, you should be attentive to how interacting with a depressed employee might make you feel. Does such a situation make you feel angry, frustrated, or diminished in your role? If so, remind yourself that the person with depression is dealing with symptoms that make every day a struggle. This is not about you. This is about how you, as a manager, can step up and help your employee. Keep in mind that depression is an illness. In most cases, it is also time-limited. By helping an employee with depression, you help the employee, your team, your company, and demonstrate strong leadership.

Kristen Bell DeTienne is a professor in the Marriott School of Management at Brigham Young University, where she teaches MBA negotiation classes. Her research examines the interdependent behavior among organizational employees, leaders, and external constituencies, such as customers. As a consultant, she has worked with a variety of organizations, including Cisco, Vivint, eBay, and Zions Bancorp.

Jill M. Hooley is a professor of psychology at Harvard University. She is also the head of the experimental psychopathology and clinical psychology program at Harvard.

Cristian Larrocha is an adviser for talent and culture at Dell Technologies, with a focus on leadership development. He received his MBA from Brigham Young University and has worked in HR strategy and operations at HP, Vivint Smart Home, and Dell Technologies.

Annsheri Reay is a student scholar in the Marriott School of Business at Brigham Young University.

NOTES

1. "Mental Health by the Numbers," National Alliance on Mental Illness, n.d., https://www.nami.org/mhstats.
2. Hillary Hoffower, "Depression Is on the Rise Among Millennials, but 20% of Them Aren't Seeking Treatment—and It's Likely Because They Can't Afford It," *Business Insider*, June 4, 2019, https://www.businessinsider.com/depression-increasing-among-millennials-gen-z-healthcare-burnout-2019-6.

3. Judy Martin and Kristi Hedges, "Tackling Depression at Work as a Productivity Strategy," *Forbes*, October 23, 2012, https://www.forbes.com/sites/work-in-progress/2012/10/23/tackling-depression-at-work-as-a-productivity-strategy/#258e6bf12294.

4. Carsten C. Schermuly and Bertolt Meyer, "Good Relationships at Work: The Effects of Leader–Member Exchange and Team–Member Exchange on Psychology Empowerment, Emotional Exhaustion, and Depression," *Journal of Organizational Behavior* 37, no. 5 (2015): 673–691, https://onlinelibrary.wiley.com/doi/abs/10.1002/job.2060.

5. Collie W. Conoley et al., "Predictors of Client Implementation of Counselor Recommendation," *Journal of Counseling Psychology* 41, no. 1 (1994): 3–7, https://psycnet.apa.org/record/1994-22305-001.

CHAPTER 14

Being Anxious When You're the Boss

by Morra Aarons-Mele

Anxiety has a purpose. It protects us from harm. Psychologist Rollo May first wrote in 1977: "We are no longer prey to tigers and mastodons but to damage to our self-esteem, ostracism by our group, or the threat of losing out in the competitive struggle. The form of anxiety has changed, but the experience remains relatively the same." In other words, even though humans today aren't chased by predators, we are chased by uncertainty about the health of our loved ones, whether we'll have a

Adapted from "Leading Through Anxiety," on hbr.org, May 11, 2020 (product #H05LK7).

job next week or next year, whether our company will go bankrupt—worries that provoke the same neurological and physical responses.

The good news for those of us who have managed anxiety for a long time is that we can learn to turn it to our advantage. Data shows that anxious people process threats differently, using regions of the brain responsible for action. We react quickly in the face of danger. We may also be more comfortable with uncomfortable feelings. When channeled thoughtfully, anxiety can motivate us to make our teams more resourceful, productive, and creative. It can break down barriers and create new bonds. But left unchecked, anxiety distracts us, zaps our energy, and drives us to make poor decisions. Anxiety is a powerful enemy, so we must make it our partner.

If you're a manager, how can you lead with authority and strength when you feel anxious? How can you inspire and motivate others when your mind and heart are racing? And if you hide the fear in an attempt to be leaderlike, where does it go? Let's walk through a four-step process for answering these questions: identifying your anxiety, taking action to manage it, limiting anxiety's impact on your leadership, and building a support infrastructure.

Acknowledging and Accepting Your Emotions

A common coping mechanism for leaders is to push through stress, fatigue, and fear. But that's succeeding *in spite of* your emotions, when it's far better to thrive *because of* your emotions. You have to learn to accept your anxiety—even though this may seem uncomfortable or counterintuitive.

Label what you're feeling

Angela Neal-Barnett, an award-winning psychologist, expert on anxiety among African Americans, and author of *Soothe Your Nerves*, is a firm believer in being honest with yourself. When you name the feeling—by saying to yourself "I'm anxious"—you can begin to address it. You can learn how anxiety informs your behavior and your decisions and what causes it to surge, which will equip you to manage it.

No one has to hear you say it. This is for you. Let yourself experience the discomfort of fear and anxiety. Play out worst-case scenarios in your head. Allow your imagination to go wild with catastrophe. Experiencing that discomfort may not be easy, but it will be worthwhile. Decades of research on emotional intelligence have shown that people who understand their own feelings have higher job satisfaction, stronger job performance, and better relationships; are more innovative; and can synthesize diverse opinions and lessen conflict. And all those things make people better leaders.

Play detective

Once you've labeled your anxiety, you can start pinpointing when it appears and why. Your triggers might be small. You might notice a stomach flip and a spark of dread when you see someone's name pop up in your inbox. Or they might be bigger. When the stock market is in turmoil, you might feel worried about what it means for your retirement account and ability to support your family in the future.

When an interaction or a situation sets you off, examine why and how you react when triggered. I call these anxiety reactions "tells." Social worker and therapist Carolyn Glass suggests asking yourself, "How did I respond to that anxiety in that moment? And were those behaviors helpful or not? Did those behaviors fuel or alleviate my anxiety?" Glass says that writing down your fears will help you examine them.

Many successful leaders react to anxiety by working harder. Your tells may also be physical. Anxiety can manifest itself as tightness in the chest, shallow breathing, clenched jaw muscles, frozen shoulders, gastrointestinal symptoms, skin breakouts, appetite changes, and radical shifts in energy. Pay attention to what your specific reactions are.

Sort out the probable from the possible

Once you understand your triggers and tells, you can start developing a new relationship with your anxiety.

Remember, some anxiety is rational and helpful. In an economic downturn it makes sense for a leader to feel anxious. You might have to lay people off. Your business might fail. But you might find that you get stuck in a negative thought loop that prevents you from moving forward; you start obsessing.

So how do you avoid being stuck? Here I turn to advice from Jerry Colonna, the leadership coach and CEO of Reboot: "Differentiate what's possible from what's probable. It is *possible* that everyone I love will die of a pandemic and I will lose everything I hold dear. But it's not *probable* that everything that we love and hold dear will disappear." Try to distinguish your worst fears from what is likely to happen. This will help calm you and give you space to move forward. So when a catastrophic thought comes into your head, such as "I'm going to mess up this project and get fired," remember that you're an unreliable narrator when you're anxious. Check in with someone you trust and ask for that person's help in separating what is likely to unfold from what is a long shot.

Taking Action to Manage Your Anxiety

Once you make your way through these three tasks, you can start to manage your anxiety daily in ways that allow you to grow as a leader and be more resourceful and productive.

The following tactics can help ground you.

Control what you can

Many faith traditions teach us to accept what we cannot control, without preoccupation or panic. But in the middle of an anxiety attack at work, you probably don't have time for philosophy. So here's what to do when things feel completely off the rails.

Structure your time

A solid body of research shows that your attitude toward how you organize and value your time has a positive impact on mental health.[1] And it's especially crucial when you're gripped by anxiety.

First thing in the morning, create a to-do list and a detailed schedule for your day. You might use 30-minute increments to spell out when you'll take a lunch break, make a phone call, or tackle that report that needs to get done. This is what many experts call "timeboxing." While you're at it, try to avoid what cognitive behavioral therapy terms "cognitive distortions." These are the catastrophic thoughts, self-judgments, and all-or-nothing ideas that often accompany anxiety.

Be careful not to overschedule or overestimate your productivity; instead, focus on the critical work and leave time to take care of yourself.

Take small, meaningful actions

When you feel anxious, an immediate task can easily become overwhelming. Take running a cash flow analysis for your business. When you open up the accounting software, your mind might go to a dark place, and all of a sudden a month's worth of figures have spiraled into the business tanking and you losing your home. To break that mental spiral, take a small, meaningful action. If running a cash flow projection terrifies you, organize some receipts or clean up some file folders until the panic subsides.

In general, focus on the near term whenever you can. You may feel anxious about what will happen—to you, your team, your family, the business—next year, or even three months from now. You can't be sure everything will be OK. But you *can* tackle tasks that have to get done this week. Focus on that, and then deal with the big questions when you feel calmer or when you can get input from trusted colleagues. Sometimes you have to turn off the future for a little while and just manage through the present.

Develop techniques for situations you can't control

Of course, it's not always possible to turn off the future. What if your board needs those cash flow projections in the next 30 minutes and you're in a downward spiral? Here you'll want to have tools that help you calm down quickly so that you can get your job done.

Find a mindfulness technique that eases your acute anxiety

There are lots of ways to do this; the key is to find what's most effective for you. One option is to focus on your breathing. Belly breaths are a classic technique. Others prefer what's called "the 4-7-8 method." Either is simple to memorize and subtle enough to do at your desk. When you deliberately slow your breath, it sends a message to your brain to calm down, and your brain then sends the message to your body so that many of the physical symptoms of anxiety—such as increased heart rate and higher blood pressure—decrease.

You can also shift your attention, which is helpful when you're having trouble focusing. Focus first on your anxiety, and then slowly turn your attention to something tangible, something you hold in your hand, like a book. By concentrating on an object in the present moment, you can turn the volume of your worry down until it's background noise. Experiment with what works for you and then keep that tactic in your back pocket for when you need it.

Compartmentalize or postpone your worry

Sometimes I talk out loud to my anxiety, saying, "Sorry, I'm going to deal with you after I finish my work." You may want to write the worry down and save it for a specific time—maybe later that day or your next session with your therapist.

In times of crisis you may actually find that things that worried you in the past fade into the background. The urgency of what's happening in the moment takes over. To stop your anxiety from sneaking into the foreground, you might tell it, "You can stay where you are. I'm part of the solution here, and I need to get this task done."

Finally, if anxiety is persistent and hampering your days, you might consider consulting a therapist or mental health professional. Talking to someone trained in helping others manage anxiety may give you additional coping mechanisms to address debilitating symptoms.

Limiting Anxiety's Impact on Your Leadership

Once you have a better sense of how you experience anxiety and how you can manage it daily, it's time to turn to how it affects your leadership and management abilities.

Make good decisions

Anxiety can impair our judgment. It can cause us to focus on the wrong things, distort the facts, or rush to conclusions. Ideally, we could postpone critical decisions until we're in a better frame of mind, but that's not always possible.

In anxious times it's important to proactively set yourself up to make good choices. Much as you do when separating the possible from the probable, start by acknowledging that your emotions can make you an unreliable narrator and that you will likely be prone to negative thoughts. Let's say you're prepping for a speech and the last time you spoke to a group of a similar size, you felt that you bombed. Ask yourself: Are you being objective? If you're not sure, check whether your memory is correct, perhaps by asking a colleague who was in the room for feedback. Of course, you need to ask the right people. Ultimately, every leader should develop a team of "real talk" peers: people who will provide their unvarnished opinions.

Practice healthy communication

One of the most dangerous aspects of anxiety is that it's contagious, and leaders set the tone. If you're not admitting that you're anxious but instead emitting irritability or distraction, you're not doing your staff any favors. But how can you be honest with your people in a way that doesn't strike fear into them? What degree of emotion is appropriate to express?

Self-aware leaders know when it's appropriate to be vulnerable. Admitting "I'm anxious today" or "I didn't sleep well" lets everyone else in the room breathe a little easier. ("Phew, it's not my fault he is so tense.") And remember, you don't have to share details; just share the state you're in. Plus, nothing establishes trust more effectively than the emotional connection fostered through empathy and shared humanity. This is why being open about your own anxiety can be so powerful. It builds

143

trust when you can ask teammates, "How are you?" and they don't feel as if they have to lie or put on a happy face, because they know you feel the strain, too.

Building a Support System

The final step in leading through anxiety is making sure you have ongoing support. This means not only surrounding yourself with the right people but also developing routines that help you deal with bouts of anxiety and lay the groundwork for maintaining your mental health.

Schedule, structure, and scenario-plan

When you have anxiety, you need to be intentional about what your days look like, as I discussed earlier. The methods are basic: making lists, prioritizing, and breaking work into manageable chunks. Chop tasks that make you extremely anxious into bearable pieces.

Also, use the detective work you did about your triggers to prepare for situations or events you know will cause you anxiety. If you're afraid of flying, mentally rehearse a business trip from "I'm going to pack" to "I'm going to order a cab and call my friend while I'm on my way to the airport" to "I'll buy M&M's when I get there because they make me happy." And finally, once on the plane: "I'm going to take a Xanax, do a calming meditation, and survive."

Know who your "safe team" is

Since you want to spare your employees the messy details of your anxiety, you need a place for those emotions to go. Make sure you have a "safe team" of people to whom you can confess scary thoughts. They can include a therapist, a coach, a mentor, a spouse or partner, and friends. It could be an intimate group of fellow leaders, online or off-line, who commit to sharing in confidence and making space for one another's difficult emotions.

Practice self-care

I don't need to belabor this point. You know what self-care means for you, whether it's sleep, exercise, hobbies, massage, spending time alone, or being with people you love. The point is, take it seriously, as if your doctor had written you a prescription for it. It's neither frivolous nor optional for you as a leader. And aspects of it you feel comfortable sharing can benefit your team: When you model good practices, others feel permission to take care of themselves, too. This could be as simple as letting people know that you don't take your phone upstairs when you head to bed, that you're taking an hour during the workday to exercise, or that you're limiting exposure to news or Twitter.

Putting in place the support infrastructure to manage your anxiety will help you ride out setbacks and tough times. It's a strategy for long-term success and sustainability as a leader. It means you'll have better workdays, both when things are status quo and during transitions and tough times.

Whether you have a diagnosed anxiety disorder or are having your first dance with this intense emotion, you can still be an effective leader. But I'll be blunt: If you don't look your anxiety in the face at some point, it will take you down. This isn't easy, but doing it will change your life and your ability to lead others for the better.

Ultimately, anxiety comes with the job of being a leader. But the process of managing it can make you stronger, more empathetic, and more effective. It might be bumpy along the way, so remember to treat yourself with compassion. Recognize that you're doing the best you can, that your emotions are normal, and that the healthiest thing you can do is to allow yourself to experience them.

———

Morra Aarons-Mele is an entrepreneur and communications executive who founded the award-winning strategic communications agency Women Online and The Mission List, an influencer database. Morra is an expert in online marketing who has been working with women online. She helped Hillary Clinton log on for her first internet chat, and has launched digital campaigns for former President Obama, Malala Yousafzai, the United Nations, and many other leading figures and organizations. An extremely anxious introvert herself, Morra hosts top-rated podcast *The Anxious Achiever* for HBR Presents from *Harvard Business Review*. She's passionate about helping people rethink the relationship between their mental health and their leadership.

NOTE

1. Ping Wang and Xiaochun Wang, "Effect of Time Management Training on Anxiety, Depression, and Sleep Quality," *Iranian Journal of Public Health* 47, no. 12 (2018): 1822–1831, https://www.ncbi.nlm.nih.gov/pmc/articles/PMC6379615/.

Helping Colleagues Who Are Struggling

.

CHAPTER 15

When You're Worried About a Colleague

by Amy Gallo

Your usually dependable colleague is missing deadlines, failing to get their work done, disappearing for long periods of time, or suddenly prone to outbursts and other erratic behavior. You may wonder what exactly is going on. Could it be anxiety, depression, or something else? How do you address what's happening—and should you? How can you be a caring colleague without trying to play the role of psychologist?

Adapted from "When You're Worried About a Colleague's Mental Health," on hbr.org, December 18, 2015 (product #H02KNM).

What the Experts Say

It's very likely that you work with someone who has a mental health issue. And because most conditions are moderate and can be treated effectively, people who are afflicted still go to the office. "In our society, people work through illnesses. They show up when they have the flu and when they're depressed," says Annie McKee, senior fellow at the University of Pennsylvania Graduate School of Education and author of *How to Be Happy at Work*. "Many people who suffer from a diagnosable condition lead productive lives. They do that by coming to terms with what's going on and treating it," says Anna Ranieri, a licensed therapist, executive coach, and coauthor of *How Can I Help?* Not all people get help, however, and it may be that your colleague has an "undetected, undiagnosed, or untreated mental health issue," explains McKee. If you suspect they might be suffering from a mental condition and it's affecting your work, here's some advice.

Don't make knee-jerk diagnoses

"It's human nature to try to find a pattern and label it," says Ranieri, but a lot of people jump to the conclusion that something's wrong before they have all the facts. "Most of us aren't trained to diagnose someone." And our speculations are often misguided. "When we see someone acting outside of the norm—erratic behavior, big mood swings, missing deadlines, not showing up to work—we often make judgments, assuming it's a mental health issue when it may be that someone's just different," says McKee. You can test the waters a bit to see if perhaps this is just the person's way of working. Ranieri suggests you say something like, "I usually keep in touch frequently about a project and I notice that there are times when you're out of reach. How can we best work together so that we're on the same page?" You may find out that there is no emotional issue and that the other person just has a different style. Don't feel like you have to label every behavior you don't understand.

"A person can be a caring colleague without being an amateur psychologist," says Ranieri. However, if your coworker doesn't give you an explanation, or you find that they are "habitually violating the norm over and over and you've determined that it's not a cultural or perspective issue, you might wonder if something more serious is going on," says McKee.

Look at your own behavior

Sometimes one of the best signs that something serious is going on with a colleague is whether their behavior is affecting the way others conduct themselves around the office. Emotions are contagious. "A good clue is that the people around the individual are spinning. Relationships are broken or people who normally don't fight are having disagreements," explains McKee. "You may start to feel down, especially when you're with the person. Or perhaps you're usually calm and you find yourself more volatile. We catch the emotional tone of the other person."

Know the limits of your relationship

If you have reason to suspect your colleague might be struggling with anxiety, depression, or another mental health issue, first think about whether you're the right person to say anything. "Part of the decision on how to handle it is understanding your relationship," says Ranieri. "If you have a close friendship with your co-worker, then this is likely something you can bring up." But if you don't, think carefully about what your role should be. As a manager, if the person's behavior is affecting their or others' work, you have an obligation to say something. (More on that later.) If you're a peer or a direct report, and you don't consider the person a friend, then it's probably not your place to address it. That doesn't mean you can't offer guidance if your colleague asks for it, but just be cognizant that you're not overstepping boundaries.

Make an observation

If you decide to broach the subject, don't come out and ask, "Are you depressed? Are you having some mental health problems?" The individual may not be ready or willing to talk about it. Instead, focus on the work and the impact their behavior is having on you and others. Make an observation like, "We've been trying to get this project done and it's been hard with you out of the office." Then, "give the person the opportunity to respond and share with you what's going on. You may learn that they're having a tough time at home, have an elderly parent who's ill, or they may say, 'I'm having trouble getting the energy to get to work every day,'" says Ranieri. If you're good friends, you can ask, "Are you all right? Is there anything I can to do help?" advises McKee. Be sure to follow the person's lead. If they open up, let them decide how much to tell you. If they say, "I'm just having a difficult time and I can't really go into it now," then don't push.

Listen

One of the most helpful things you can do for someone struggling with a mental health issue is to listen. If your colleague decides to open up about "temporary problems or long-term psychological issues," just sitting down and hearing them out "can be beneficial to them," says Ranieri. "It helps to know that people recognize the condition but are not judging them for having it." And this may be all you do for the colleague. "You're not giving advice. You can offer your own experience if it's relevant—'I went through a hard time and this is what I did'—but you're not telling them what to do and you're not making it all about you," she says.

When to talk to someone else

Generally, you want to keep your observations and discussions confidential. But there are two situations in which you may want to enlist the help of others. The first is when the "behavior is so unpredictable and frightening that you're worried they might be putting themselves or others at danger," says Ranieri. The second is when you believe talking to the person directly would put you at risk. Perhaps you're worried about their reaction, or they're your boss and you worry it will change your relationship.

"That's where you might talk with HR or the person's manager if you feel the third party will handle it appropriately and confidentially," Ranieri says. Express your concern in terms of the work—for example: "There's be-havior I don't understand and it's having a negative im-pact on me and my ability to get my work done." This can be hard to do, of course. "There's a cultural taboo about being a snitch," says McKee. "But if you're at risk of fail-ing at your job, or the environment is becoming toxic, it's your responsibility to go to someone who can help." Re-member, you're trying to help. "If we suspect that there's a real problem, shouldn't we try to get them the support they need?" she says.

You also have to protect yourself from any negative consequences. If you fear the person's behavior will put your job or reputation at risk, McKee suggests docu-menting what's happening. Write down what you've done—emails you've sent, conversations you've had, re-quests you've made. "These situations can come back to haunt you if you're not careful about it. Sometimes it's cut and dry: 'They didn't show up to the meeting again.' But also document what might seem off to you: 'They yelled in a meeting,'" advises McKee.

Put up boundaries if necessary

There can be downsides to offering help. "You can't be-come a de facto therapist," McKee warns. "It's fine to have a conversation, but you need to be ready to steer the person toward professional help if that's what they need." Ranieri agrees: If the person keeps coming back to you for advice and support, "cordially say, 'Thanks for relay-ing this to me, but I'm not an expert. I'm rooting for you but I'm not the person to delve into that.'"

Create a caring culture

If you're a manager, focus on fostering a safe environment where people can talk about these sorts of issues. "Many managers may want to avoid conversations around health, mental health, and emotional well-being," says McKee. But you shouldn't. If people aren't getting their work done or are preventing others from doing so, you have a responsibility to do something about it. You can talk to the person, explain the impact on the work, and ask how you might help. You might refer the person to your employee assistance program or ask your HR department for help.

If you've struggled with a mental health issue in the past or have a family member who has, consider talking about it at work, if and only if you feel safe. "Most people don't want to say, 'I suffer from depression,' because there's a shame about psychological issues," Ranieri acknowledges, but the more you talk openly about it, the more you build awareness and take away the stigma, paving the way for others to get help.

Case Study: Make the Person Feel Safe

Several years ago, when Barbara Ricci was a managing director at UBS, she suspected something was going on with a longtime client, George (not his real name). When they worked closely together on his firm's investment portfolio, talked on the phone, and dined out, she noticed a pattern of behavior: He would act differently at certain points—talk more loudly, more quickly—and because of her work as the president of the board at the National Alliance on Mental Illness–New York City and her relationship with a brother who'd been diagnosed with schizophrenia, Barbara thought George might be having manic episodes. Initially, this didn't concern her much because it didn't affect their work and she assumed he was managing his condition. But she did talk openly about her own family experience and tried to give him "a safe space to confide," she recalls.

But then things got more serious. "I noticed uncharacteristic trading patterns in his portfolio. He wasn't taking prudent risk," she explains. Since George was in charge of billions of dollars and making large, "inappropriate" transactions, Barbara felt she had to say something.

She called George away from the trading desk and asked him if he was OK. He waved off her question and said he had no idea what she was talking about. Although she'd wanted to deal with him directly, offering him help and resources, she quickly realized how difficult it would be to get through to him at this time, so she went to his manager, a person she trusted to do the right thing. "He was very open-minded, and I knew he'd handle the situation appropriately and keep our conversation confidential."

George's manager was caught off guard—he hadn't realized his employee was struggling. But he talked to him, explaining that George seemed stressed out and should take the rest of the week off. Barbara doesn't know what George did that week, but after a brief respite, he came back to his position full-time and behaved in a much more stable way. "He stayed in that role for a number of years and continued to be very good at his job," Barbara reports.

Eventually he left and took another job, but years later, he called Barbara to say that he was struggling again and remembered that she'd talked to him about mental health issues in the past. She welcomed the opportunity to offer advice and resources because he'd asked for them. "I was happy to be able to help," she says.

———

Amy Gallo is a contributing editor at *Harvard Business Review* and the author of the *HBR Guide to Dealing with Conflict at Work* and *Getting Along: How to Work with Anyone (Even Difficult People)*. Her years of therapy have informed her thinking on interpersonal dynamics between coworkers and helped her better navigate the stress and anxiety of work. Follow her on Twitter @amyegallo.

CHAPTER 16

Noticing and Responding to Microaggressions

by Ella F. Washington

We've all been in situations at work when someone says or does something that feels hostile or offensive to some aspect of our identity—and the person doesn't even realize it. These kinds of actions—insensitive statements, questions, or assumptions—are called "microaggressions," and they can target many aspects of who we are. For example, they could be related to someone's race, gender, sexuality, parental status, socioeconomic background, mental health, or any other aspect of our identity.

Most often, microaggressions are aimed at traditionally marginalized identity groups. Yet these hurtful actions can happen to anyone, of any background, at any professional level. A microaggression against a Black woman, for example, could be a statement such as "You aren't like the other Black people I know" (indicating the person is different from stereotypes of Black people), whereas one for a white male might be, "Oh, you don't ever have to worry about fitting in" (indicating that all white men are always comfortable and accepted). Essentially, microaggressions are based on a simple, damaging idea: "Because you are X, you probably are/are not or like/don't like Y."

One criticism of discourse about microaggressions is that our society has become "hypersensitive" and that casual remarks are now blown out of proportion. However, research is clear about the impact seemingly innocuous statements can have on one's physical and mental health, especially over the course of an entire career: increased rates of depression, prolonged stress and trauma, physical concerns like headaches, high blood pressure, and difficulties with sleep.[1] Further, the reality of the Great Resignation has employers paying closer attention to how organizational culture can influence whether or not employees want to leave. One study found that 7 in 10 workers said they would be upset by a microaggression, and half said the action would make them consider leaving their job.[2]

So the reality is that microaggressions are not so micro in terms of their impact. They should be taken seriously, because at their core they signal disrespect and reflect inequality.[3]

To create inclusive, welcoming, and healthy workplaces, we must actively combat microaggressions. Doing so requires understanding how they show up and how to respond productively to them, whether they happen to us or to colleagues. Inclusive work environments are not just nice to have—they positively contribute to employee well-being and mental and physical health.[4]

It's important to note that building inclusive workplaces requires candid, authentic conversations on tough subjects, like sexism, homophobia, and racism—and it's natural to worry that we may commit microaggressions in these kinds of conversations by saying the wrong thing. The more awareness we have about how microaggressions show up, the more we can work toward decreasing them in the workplace. Yet the reality is that we all make mistakes, so you should know what to do if you witness a microaggression or commit one.

As I share in my forthcoming book about DEI, *The Necessary Journey*, awareness is always the first step. Here are some ways to become more aware of microaggressions, interrupt them when we see them, and promote workplace cultures with fewer microaggressions.

Being More Aware of Microaggressions

There are many words and phrases in the English language that are rooted in systemically favoring dominant groups in society. Thus many parts of our everyday speech have historical roots in racism, sexism, and other forms of discrimination. For example, the following terms you may casually hear in the workplace have hurtful connotations:

- "Blacklist" refers to a list of things that are seen negatively, juxtaposed against "whitelist," a list of things that are seen positively.[5]

- "Man up" equates gender with strength or competence.

- "Peanut gallery" originated in the 1800s and referred to the sections of segregated theaters usually occupied by Black people.[6]

These words and phrases can trigger thoughts of current and past discrimination for people. Taking time to be intentional with the language you use is part of treating each other with respect. While it's unrealistic to know every cultural minefield that may exist in language, the goal is to be thoughtful about the origins of common phrases and, more importantly, to change your use of these terms if you become aware that they are problematic. For example, if you are looking to encourage someone, telling them to "rise to the moment" or "be brave" is a better way to communicate the sentiment than "man up." It takes work to unlearn the many fraught words and phrases in our cultural lexicon, but most people find it's not that difficult to do once they set their minds to actively being more inclusive.

Here are examples of a few types of microaggressions that you may hear within and outside the workplace:

- Race

  - "I didn't realize you were Jewish—you don't look Jewish," signaling that a person of the Jewish heritage has a stereotypical look. (Of course, similar statements happen to people from many backgrounds.)

- "I believe the most qualified person should get the job," signaling that someone is being given an unfair advantage because of their race.

- Citizenship

  - "Your English is so good—where are your parents from?" signaling that people with English as a second language are generally less capable of speaking English.

  - "But where are you *really* from?" signaling that where someone grew up isn't their "true" origin. This microaggression often happens to people who are in ethnic and racial minorities, whom others assume are immigrants.

- Class

  - "How did you get into that school?" signaling that someone's background makes them an anomaly at a prestigious school.

  - "You don't seem like you grew up poor," signaling that someone from a particular socioeconomic background should look or behave a certain way.

- Mental health

  - "That's insane" or "That's crazy," using terminology related to a mental health condition to describe surprise or astonishment.

- "You don't seem like you are depressed. Sometimes I get sad too," minimizing the experiences of people with mental illness.

- "Don't mind my OCD!" using the acronym for obsessive compulsive disorder, a mental health condition where an individual is plagued by obsessive thoughts and fears that can lead to compulsions, to describe attention to detail, fastidiousness, or being organized.

- Gender

  - "Don't be so sensitive," signaling that someone, likely a woman, is being "too emotional" in a situation where a man would be more objective.

  - "Thanks, sweetheart" and similar comments often directed at women, which are often not appreciated or even offensive.

- Sexuality

  - "That's so gay" to mean something is bad or undesirable, signaling that being gay is associated with negative and undesirable characteristics.

  - "Do you have a wife/husband?" which assumes heteronormative culture and behaviors, versus more inclusive phrasing such as "Do you have a partner?"

- Parental status

  - "You don't have kids to pick up, so you can work later, right?" signaling that someone without children does not have a life outside of work.

In the workplace, microaggressions can happen in all types of conversations. For example, they may occur during hiring when someone is evaluating a candidate with a different demographic background than their own, during the performance evaluation process when someone is highlighting the positive or negative aspects of an employee, or in customer service when someone is interacting with customers who have a different first language than their own. We should all become more aware of microaggressions in general, but in professional environments there should be a special level of attention to and care taken in the language we use.

Responding to Microaggressions

The more you increase your awareness of microaggressions, the more you will inevitably notice they are happening—and wonder how or if you should intercede. As with the advice given to victims of a microaggression, you have the option to respond in the moment or later on, or let it go.

There is no right approach to dealing with microaggressions, but here are a few considerations for when you witness one:

1. **What's the right moment to say something?** Consider the environment and be thoughtful about

how to create a safe space for the conversation. Think about whether the conversation is best had in the moment (possibly in front of other people) or one-on-one. In some situations, an in-the-moment approach may be sufficient. For example, if someone accidentally misgenders a colleague in a meeting, a leader could say, "Let's make sure we are using everyone's correct pronouns," and keep the meeting going. Doing this can make it less taboo to point out microaggressions and help to create a culture of positive in-the-moment correction when they happen. But no one likes to be put on the spot, and conversations are much more likely to turn tense if your colleague feels like you are calling them out. So if you need to confront someone, try to "call them in" by creating a safe environment where you can engage the person in honest, authentic dialogue—without a client or other colleagues present—to say, "Hey, I know you didn't mean it this way, but let's not use language like . . ."

2. **What's your relationship to the person who made the comment?** Do you have a personal relationship with the person who committed the microaggression? If so, you might be able to simply say, "Hey, you made a comment earlier that did not sit well with me." However, if you do not have a personal relationship with the colleague, you may want to consider what you know about their personality (do they tend to

be combative?) and history with uncomfortable conversations (are they generally approachable?). You may also need to bring in other colleagues they are closer with.

3. **What's your personal awareness of the micro-aggression's subject?** Be honest about your level of familiarity with the subject at hand. For example, maybe you recognize that a comment is a racial microaggression, but you do not know the history or full implications of it. In that case, it's OK to talk to the person, but recognize you are not an authority on the topic, and consider learning more first or talking to someone who has more familiarity with the topic.

Once you realize a microaggression has been committed, and you decide to act, remind your colleagues of the difference between *intent* and *impact*. While the speaker may not have intended the comment to be offensive, we must acknowledge the impact of our statements. Intent does not supersede or excuse actual impact. For example, you could say to the person, "I know you may have intended your statement to come off as _____, but the way I received it was _____." Sometimes simply highlighting the gap between intent and impact can be enlightening for the other person.

If You Realize You Have Committed a Microaggression

If someone tells you that you have said something offensive, this is an obvious moment to pause and consider the best way to handle the situation. Using your emotional intelligence, here are some steps to take:

- **Take a moment to pause.** Being called out can put us on the defensive, so breathe deeply and remember that everyone makes mistakes. In most cases committing a microaggression does not mean you are bad person; it signals that you have a chance to treat a colleague with greater respect and to grow on your DEI journey. Taking a moment to pause, breathe, and reflect can help you avoid reacting with emotion and potentially saying something rash that could make the situation worse.

- **Ask for clarification.** If you are unsure what you did to offend your colleague, invite dialogue by asking for clarification. Say, "Could you say more about what you mean by that?"

- **Listen for understanding.** Listen to your colleague's perspective, even when you disagree. Far too often in uncomfortable conversations, we listen for the opportunity to speak and insert our own opinions instead of truly listening for understanding. To make sure you have understood your colleague's point of view, you could restate or paraphrase what you heard: "I think I heard you saying _____ [paraphrase their comments]. Is that correct?"

- **Acknowledge and apologize.** Once you process that harm has been done, you must acknowledge the offense and sincerely apologize for your statement. This is a moment to be honest, whether you lacked the knowledge of a certain word's history or made a comment that was insensitive. You could say something like, "I can now better understand how I was wrong in this situation. I will work to become more aware of _____ [the topic that you need to increase your cultural awareness of]."

- **Create space for follow-up.** The majority of these tough conversations take more than one discussion to work through. Allow yourself and your colleagues the opportunity to follow up in the future to continue the conversation, especially when cooler heads can prevail. You may say something like, "I would be happy to talk about this more in the future if you have any follow-up thoughts. I appreciate you taking the time to share your perspective with me."

What Leaders Should Know

While microaggressions often happen at the individual level, companies that say they are committed to inclusion should have zero tolerance for exclusionary or discriminatory language toward any employee. Leaders should set the standard by providing training on topics such as microaggressions. Yet, because of the insidious nature of microaggressions, leaders and HR professionals have the responsibility to correct individuals when they become aware that these offenses have happened.

Many microaggressions can become part of an organization's culture if not corrected. For example, I have worked with some organizations where confusing two people of the same race happened often and was casually overlooked as an honest mistake. While we all do make mistakes, when these same types of incidents happen consistently to the same groups of people, leaders need to correct the behavior. One client came to me with the issue that two Asian women on the same team were often called each other's name, giving them a feeling of interchangeability. I helped the client share with the firm some tools on how to politely correct someone in the moment, as well as provided some general reminders to the firm about why it's offensive to confuse two people of the same race. One thing that firm did was to push employees to learn each other's names and make sure to have individual interactions with new colleagues to get to know them. They even had a name challenge, with a prize, when they returned to the office after working remotely during the pandemic. In this way, the firm acted to not only call out inappropriate behavior but also shift the culture by making it clear that knowing colleagues' names was a key expectation for all team members.

Ultimately, getting better at noticing and responding to microaggressions—and at being more aware of our everyday speech—is a journey, one with a real effect on our mental health and well-being at work. Microaggressions affect everyone, so creating more inclusive and culturally competent workplace cultures means each of us must explore our own biases in order to become aware of them. The goal is not to be fearful of communicating with each other, but instead to embrace the opportunity to be intentional about it. Creating inclusive cultures where people can thrive does not happen overnight. It takes a continuous process of learning, evolving, and growing.

———————

Ella F. Washington is a professor of practice at Georgetown University's McDonough School of Business; the founder of Ellavate Solutions, which provides diversity and inclusion strategy and training for organizations; the author of *The Necessary Journey: Making Real Progress on Equity and Inclusion* (Harvard Business Review Press), and the cohost of *Cultural Competence*, a weekly podcast sponsored by Gallup's Center on Black Voices. Ella believes strongly in the power of therapy and has seen a therapist for the past three years. She also seeks leadership coaching to help her continue to grow and navigate the challenges of everyday work and life.

NOTES

1. "Understanding Racial Microaggression and Its Effect on Mental Health, Pfizer," n.d., https://www.pfizer.com/news/articles/under standing_racial_microaggression_and_its_effect_on_mental_health.

2. Jillesa Gebhardt, "Study: Microaggressions in the Workplace," SurveyMonkey, n.d., https://www.surveymonkey.com/curiosity/micro aggressions-research/.

3. "Offer Employees the Flexibility to Fit Work into Their Lives," Lean In, n.d., https://leanin.org/women-in-the-workplace-report -2018/offer-employees-the-flexibility-to-fit-work-into-their-lives.

4. Ben C. Fletcher, "Diversity and Inclusiveness Is Good for Your Well-Being," *Psychology Today*, September 18, 2016, https://www .psychologytoday.com/us/blog/do-something-different/201609/ diversity-and-inclusiveness-is-good-your-well-being.

5. Frank Houghton and Sharon Houghton, "'Blacklists' and 'Whitelists': A Salutary Warning Concerning the Prevalence of Racist

Language in Discussion of Predatory Publishing," *Journal of the Medical Library Association* 106, no. 4 (2018): 527–530, https://www.ncbi.nlm.nih.gov/pmc/articles/PMC6148600/.

6. Olivia Eubanks, "Here Are Some Commonly Used Terms That Actually Have Racist Origins," ABC News, July 30, 2020, https://abcnews.go.com/Politics/commonly-terms-racist-origins/story?id=71840410#:~:text=told%20ABC%20News.-,Peanut%20gallery,by%20people%20with%20limited%20means.

CHAPTER 17

Being a Mental Health Ally

by Katherine Ponte

It is highly likely that you will experience a mental health challenge at some point in your life. Recognizing this possibility should motivate you to be a workplace ally for mental health, to treat your colleagues dealing with mental health issues with the empathy you would want under similar circumstances. Yet the stigma and lack of information about mental health block the way in many workplaces. The myth that people with mental health conditions cannot make meaningful contributions leads to conscious and unconscious bias. We must work together to eradicate the stigma and its devastating impacts. We may struggle with mental health, but we can recover. We can thrive at home and work, and we can help make this possible for each other by being allies, collaborating to create a supportive workplace for all.

To be a mental health ally at work is to help those struggling with mental health issues feel valued and needed. This can have positive long-term benefits, including increased employee engagement, productivity, and loyalty.[1] Strengthening and deepening relationships between colleagues can also benefit the broader employee community. When we're supported, we're also more eager to support others, creating a virtuous self-reinforcing cycle.

Some of the most effective ways you can be a mental health ally are to talk one-on-one with colleagues who are struggling, use supportive language, educate yourself and colleagues about mental health, encourage group engagement, and create policies that help employees who need it.

Talking to a Colleague One-on-One

Knowing when and how to engage with someone who may be struggling with their mental health can be difficult. Talking about mental illness isn't easy, particularly at work and particularly for people with a mental health condition. You don't want to jump to conclusions about someone or seem judgmental. You don't want to offend a colleague. And you want to respect professional and personal boundaries. It may be most challenging to speak to people who have a serious mental illness, as they are often the most stigmatized, making them extremely reluctant to talk about the issue.

Before talking to someone, listen and watch for signs that they are struggling, as well as for their potential sensitivities. For example, colleagues with serious and chronic issues may disclose their feelings but not their diagnosis. They may also experience self-stigma, or the internalization of the stigma, which can amplify the impact of others' negative beliefs. Further, people with mental illness may experience an anticipated stigma, or the belief that they will experience prejudice, discrimination, and stereotyping. For these reasons, they often have heightened sensitivity to stigma and rejection.

Keep in mind the following strategies and considerations for your conversation.

Prepare yourself

Reflecting on and correcting your implicit bias around mental health will help you be an ally to your colleagues. You may not mean to contribute to the stigma, but even an unintentional stigma is hurtful. Think about any assumptions or preconceptions you may have about mental health conditions and the people who deal with them; then discard them.

Be open and approachable with your colleague and consider sharing your own vulnerability or experience with mental health challenges. If you have this experience directly or through other relationships, talking about it to open a dialogue can be very powerful, putting you and the other person on more equal footing and showing that you are empathic and understanding. Being an ally requires patience, gentle persistence, and creativity. Don't be frustrated or discouraged if your initial efforts to talk to a colleague are unsuccessful. The goal of any conversation should be to help your coworker talk about their struggles, support them by asking whether and how you can help, and gently remind them of any benefits or resources your company or health-care plan provides.

Find a good time

If you notice a significant change in a colleague's mood or behavior, you may want to initiate a conversation. Watch for impaired concentration, missed deadlines, reduction in work quality, less communication, "worried" appearance, tardiness, and repeated unexplained absences. You might be inclined to ignore this behavior as a private matter or as something for your manager or HR to address. But if you're close with the person, you might be in the best position to identify an issue and connect with your colleague by reaching out in a friendly and caring way. Timing is important; try to pick a "good day" when your colleague seems approachable or relaxed.

Some people show no outward signs of struggle or work concerns, such as those who suffer from high-functioning anxiety. You can't always assume that someone is not struggling merely based on their appearance or work performance. Creating a workplace culture where colleagues demonstrate understanding and empathy will help people feel more comfortable reaching out or seeking support when needed. HR and managers should make resources, including a mental health handbook, available and easily accessible to all.

Start gently

Talking about mental health should be as normal as possible. Simply asking, "How are you feeling today?" or "How was your weekend?" or "How's that assignment going?" can create space for a mental health discussion. Of course, you'll want to strike an open, genuine, and empathic tone. A casual, nonconfrontational approach can facilitate a more open dialogue. Be prepared that your colleague may be defensive or try to hide their challenges. They may fear being stigmatized or becoming a topic of office gossip. So don't insist that your colleague talk with you. Instead, gently nudge them by telling them you're available to listen if and when they want to speak.

Validate the person's performance; they may experience strong self-doubt, which can be paralyzing. They may also experience imposter syndrome or feel guilty for being a "weak link" or not "keeping up" with the team. Remind them of how they were able to overcome challenging tasks in the past, reassuring them that things will be OK and making them feel valued and needed. You can also help brainstorm other ways to reduce their workload if that is negatively contributing to their mental health.

Use the right approach

Try reaching out in different ways. Starting with a face-to-face discussion may not be ideal, as people with mental health challenges may feel ashamed or embarrassed. Reaching out with a call or text message may be more effective. If you talk in person, consider whether a spot away from the office would provide more privacy. Begin the conversation by assuring that what you discuss will be kept private and confidential—and, of course, honor what you say.

After the initial discussion, continue the conversation if the person is willing to, especially if they have shared sensitive information. Many people with mental illness fear being disliked, abandoned, or rejected once others learn of their illness. So continue to have regular conversations while gently checking in. Sometimes people are more willing to talk about stressors than a mental health challenge, even if the stressor led to their challenges. For example, you can ask, "How are the kids adjusting to school?" instead of, "Are you still stressed about your kids?"

Using Supportive Language

When talking to a colleague who is or may be struggling with their mental health, always be mindful of what you're saying and how you say it. The following are a few samples of what to say and not say. Every person has their own trigger points or vulnerabilities, so stay thoughtful and considerate.

Be sensitive

Don't say: "I have to talk to you about your attitude [behavior, mood]."

Say: "You don't seem like yourself lately. Would you like to talk about it? I'll understand if you don't want to."

Don't say: "You seem to be falling behind on your work. Why can't you keep up?"

Say: "I know that work can sometimes be challenging. Is there anything I can do to help?"

Don't say: "I don't believe you are struggling; you're so strong. You'll get over this."

Say: "I suffer from _____; I've had a really hard time in the past when _____. I can't imagine what you're going through, but it seems hard."

Don't say: "Cheer up" [never use platitudes].

Say: "I hope you feel a little better tomorrow."

If you're a manager talking to someone who may benefit from a work break:

Don't say: "I think you need to have some time off."

Say: "You're a valuable member of our team. We need you, but you can take time off if it would help. We can give you part-time work, you can work from home, and you can stay connected with your colleagues" [of course, adapt this language to whatever your company policies allow].

Avoid stigma

Don't say: "You are bipolar."

Say: "You are a person with bipolar disorder" [*always* use person-first language—you would never say "You are cancer"].

Don't say: "I understand what you're going through" [unless you have mental illness; even if you do, be sensitive, as each person experiences mental illness differently].

Say: "I don't know what you're going through, but I would like to help you. Is there any way that I can?"

Encourage

Don't say: "You don't seem to be getting better."

Say: "Mental illness can be managed and treated; sometimes it just takes finding the right care team and plan. I will be here to support you. You can count on me."

Don't say: "Maybe you should try _____ and _____" [unsolicited advice is usually not welcomed].

Say: "I heard _____ can be helpful or has helped me in the past. Would you like to look into it together?"

Don't say: "You'll figure this out. You don't need any help. You're not weak."

Say: "I think it's brave that you recognize that you are struggling and willing to get help."

Cooperate

Don't say: "You have to see a doctor."

Say: "I wonder if a doctor might be able to help you. Our mental health handbook provides referrals, or you can reach out to your insurance company for help. Or maybe a therapist could be useful to you."

Don't say: "You need to focus on getting better."

Say: "We can get through this together; we are here for you."

Educating Employees About Mental Health

Education on mental health issues is the foundation for helping people be better allies. If you're a leader, encouraging or instituting better education at your company is a big-picture way you can be a mental health ally. There are two broad types of educational programs: personal accounts in an intimate gathering or auditorium environment and informational events in a workshop or classroom format.

Personal accounts

Events that feature intimate, lived experiences and personal accounts are often the most effective, as they can humanize challenges and foster empathy. Leaders in particular can share their experiences with mental health, which can also impact corporate culture and policy. Employees can share their stories, which often have the greatest impact since they're more likely to be more relatable to other employees. The speakers at these events don't have to be folks on staff. Some organizations offer experts who have experience leading these kinds of discussions.

Workshops and classes

Informational events can provide useful background knowledge to all employees. Several organizations offer workplace training, the most popular being the Mental Health First Aid Course offered by the National Council for Mental Wellbeing. Mental health nonprofits such as the National Alliance on Mental Illness–New York City (where I am on the board) also provide training. Another helpful employee resource is a mental health handbook that covers mental health basics, benefits information, and a list of vetted health-care providers. Be sure to refer employees to reputable sources such as NAMI and Mayo Clinic for additional information.

Engaging Employee Groups

Peer-to-peer contact can benefit those employees who struggle with loneliness and isolation. Employee resource groups (ERGs) can provide a forum for those impacted by, living with, or supporting someone with mental illness and identify opportunities to address any workplace issues. All employees should be welcome to join, but privacy for members should be preserved. Managers should promote and participate in these groups where relevant to help normalize these issues.

In addition to ERGs, you can model good behavior in groups by openly and publicly talking about mental health, sharing your own challenges, lobbying for good mental health for all employees at all levels, and supporting mental health activities, initiatives, and events.

Group self-care activities in the workplace promote peer-to-peer engagement. Popular activities include exercise and fitness classes, healthy meals, meditation, and mindfulness programs. These experiences also foster more in-person conversations, which can facilitate discussions about mental health. Sometimes people with mental health challenges find it comforting to do things with colleagues that aren't directly focused on mental health; many fear the loss of such social connections due to their mental health issues. Extracurricular activities organized around a shared interest or affinity can create a space in which to create connections with other employees that facilitate engagement. These may include employee involvement in DEI initiatives and discussion groups or community service programs. Sponsoring or encouraging participation in mental health nonprofit events such as fundraising walks also helps raise awareness and invites open employee discussion while benefiting programs.

Supporting Mental Health with Company Policies

Company leaders should take a multipart approach here.

Deploy a supportive mental health policy

Implementing and maintaining a strong policy against stigma and promoting mental health creates a supportive work environment and culture. Provide all employees with a clear overview of the mental health benefits your company offers. Communicate that any stigma associated with mental health will be treated in the same manner as other forms of discrimination, and encourage managers and employees to speak up against it. Also encourage employees to confront colleagues that espouse any and all stigma, whether or not intentional, and report such conduct to supervisors. Your company's mental health policy can include a transparent company commitment to best practices for addressing mental health issues. Employees should have clearly identified and available resources to report concerns and an uncomplicated complaint or feedback process that provides anonymity.

If you're in management, you can create a mental health director position to develop, implement, and enforce your company's mental health policy. A workplace mental health committee comprising a diverse group of stakeholders, especially employees living with mental illness, can help shape, implement, and maintain this policy.

Offer office accommodations

Allies and leaders should lobby for and support office accommodations that can benefit all employees by helping prevent mental health challenges and mitigating workplace stressors that can worsen mental health. Some easy and low-cost examples of accommodations from the Americans with Disabilities Act include offering late starts (many psychiatric medications can be sedating), breaks to attend medical appointments, flextime, quiet workspaces, office psychiatric service dogs (or emotional support animals), remote work, and part-time work. Encourage all employees to discuss accommodations for their team and suggestions for how best to incorporate them.

Managers should consider offering these accommodations proactively to employees in need. Assure employees that they will not experience repercussions if they ask for accommodations, and that if they disclose a mental illness it will be kept strictly confidential. Telling an employee that an illness will be "kept off the record" can be comforting. Employees with mental illnesses are entitled to reasonable accommodations under the law, but to benefit they must disclose their condition. Managers should keep in mind that many think the risks of disclosure far exceed the benefits.

Increase access to care

Offer access to good mental health care benefits, including a comprehensive package that accords physical and mental health parity. It should include coverage for a wide range of mental health services and medications. Offer generous short-term and long-term medical leave policies with clearly stipulated durations and possibilities for extensions. Leave policy should not require disclosure of specific conditions. Another beneficial measure is on-call therapy assistance (as mental health crises often occur outside the workplace). General wellness programs should also be available to all employees to ensure a positive impact on mental health. Ensure that employees are aware of these benefits through information sessions and company communication channels.

Finally, anonymous online peer-to-peer support communities that preserve confidentiality can be helpful. Many companies use mental health apps to support employees, but their effectiveness may be questionable. According to the American Psychiatric Association (APA), many apps lack evidence of their effectiveness; in addition, they may not be secure, lack adequate privacy controls, or may sell user data without appropriate disclosure or authorization. The APA has developed an evaluation model to assess associated risks and rate mental health apps.[2] Employers should carefully evaluate mental health apps for these risks and their potential effectiveness before promoting them to employees.

People with mental health challenges, no matter the severity, can thrive in the workplace and be valuable team members. Allies play an important role by helping to provide the empathy and compassion they need to overcome key challenges. Our collective will, empathy, and compassion can break down the formidable barriers of stigma. Workplace mental health initiatives can and do help. In the end, what matters most is bringing our shared humanity into the workplace.

Katherine Ponte is the founder of ForLikeMinds, a board member of the National Alliance on Mental Illness–New York City, a lecturer of psychiatry with the Program for Recovery and Community Health at Yale University's School of Medicine, a blogger for the National Alliance on Mental Illness, the author and coauthor of articles published in leading psychiatric journals, and the author of *ForLikeMinds: Mental Illness Recovery Insights.* Katherine has been living with severe bipolar I disorder with psychosis, including major depressive disorder, for over 20 years. She is now happily living in recovery.

NOTES

1. Larry Dossey, "The Helper's High," *Explore* 14, no. 6 (2018): 393–399.
2. "The App Evaluation Model," American Psychiatric Association, https://www.psychiatry.org/psychiatrists/practice/mental-health-apps/the-app-evaluation-model.

Taking Action from the C-Suite

CHAPTER 18

Living with Depression in the C-Suite

**An interview with Paul Greenberg
by Morra Aarons-Mele**

When we discuss mental health at work, we often talk about what it means for individual contributors and people lower in the org chart. But leaders in the C-suite also struggle with their mental health—as well as worries about how colleagues might view them and whether their careers might be affected if their challenges were public knowledge.

Morra Aarons-Mele, host of podcast *The Anxious Achiever*, spoke with Paul Greenberg, CEO of the

Adapted from "Battling Depression from the C-Suite," *The Anxious Achiever* podcast, season, 1 episode 8, November 18, 2019.

digital video firm Butter Works, about his decades of living through deep, chronic depression and suicidal impulses, while also finding success in a number of leadership positions. The discussion includes frank comments about suicidal thinking and electroconvulsive therapy.

Morra Aarons-Mele: Paul, you worked nearly three decades of 10-hour days, during which none of your colleagues knew that you were struggling with depression. How is that possible?

Paul Greenberg: I honestly wish I could tell you. It was brutal, but I had some ability to parcel out the work that needed to happen and contain how I felt and what I needed to get done. Sometimes the work was a solace, where I could focus on something besides the depression. Often, however, it was a slog—I really worked hard to get through it.

You were also a manager, dealing with other people's problems, leading meetings, and so on. What did those slog days feel like?

Exhausting, Sisyphean. I would get up in the morning and think, "OK, I just need to get through this day. Whatever I have to do, I'm just going to keep pushing the rock up the hill." Every day, I would have almost constant suicidal thoughts—"I want to kill myself." I wasn't visualizing actually killing myself. I just kept hearing those thoughts, and that was exhausting.

Then there was this heaviness, this pit in my stomach, which led me to catastrophize everything: "Nothing will ever work out. We'll never get through this. I'm going to lose my job and be homeless, and everything will fall apart forever."

I would get to work and focus as hard as I could on the people around me, trying to feel needed, and trying to understand and be as empathetic as possible about how I could help them. Somehow, that made it a little easier to get through the day—to feel like I was part of something bigger.

But as soon as I had any downtime when I wasn't in a meeting or I was just eating my salad at my desk, the depression would rush back and I would feel hopeless, anxious, angry, and frustrated. Then when I had to go to my next meeting, I would shake it off and push through.

Let's talk about treatment. How many meds have you tried during your life?

Probably 75. And nothing worked.

So you tried electroshock therapy five years ago? How did you and your medical treatment team decide on that? Were you afraid to try it? What happened to get you there?

I was really down, worse than I had ever been. My psychopharmacologist, who's affiliated with Columbia University, had been working with me on the meds and trying different things. Several times, he had said, "OK, I think it's time for ECT" [electroconvulsive therapy]. I thought, "I've seen *One Flew Over the Cuckoo's Nest*. No way are you getting me strapped into that thing."

They say that when you're in enough pain, you change, and finally I was in enough pain. I said, "OK, I'll do anything you suggest." He got me into the ECT outpatient program at Columbia. It's not anything like *One Flew Over the Cuckoo's Nest* anymore. They gave me a general anesthetic and a muscle relaxant. I counted backward from 100, got to 88, and then I woke up. And they had done the treatment. It's 85% effective with drug-resistant unipolar and bipolar depression, which is just amazing.

I went in three days a week for four weeks. After the 12th treatment, I was at the playground with my kids on a Sunday morning and suddenly felt happy for the first time in my adult life. I thought maybe I was having a heart attack. This albatross that had been around my neck for so long lifted, and I just felt physically and emotionally lighter, and the sun looked different, and the kids looked different. I just thought, "Wow, I am actually happy."

And the thing is, when I would sit in the outpatient waiting room, there were always a number of people there. I wasn't the only person getting ECT. It's just something people don't talk about.

Take us to the present day.

I was doing OK for a long time. The ECT allowed me to do real therapy, and I realized that I never had been able to because the depression was this big wall in my way. Some of these realizations, which were incredibly painful, were about my childhood and my life, and what's going on. That sent me into more depression, which got better, then worse, then better, and then worse.

Then it got as bad as it was before ECT. My doctor said, "OK, it's time to try ketamine." I thought, "OK, I've heard of ketamine."

It was a club drug in the early 2000s.

Actually, ketamine was invented in 1962 as an anesthetic to be used medically. Then in the late '90s, academics started looking into a use in depression. In 2000, researchers at Yale had great success with it. This year, the FDA approved a Johnson & Johnson ketamine nasal spray for depression, which is now being sold. So, it's been validated, although what Johnson & Johnson got approved was a portion of what the full ketamine drug is.

I get ketamine intravenously. I go in for 40 minutes, and I feel loopy and a little spacey for 25 minutes and then I come out of it. It works really, really fast. Within four to five hours, usually, your suicidal thoughts go away; your depression goes away. But those effects aren't long-lasting unless you do it several times. I went Monday and Friday for three weeks, and after six treatments the depression was totally gone. My suicidal thoughts are totally gone.

It's new, so the doctors don't know a lot about how to maintain the effects, but ultimately you're getting a relatively small dose, so it's not addictive. One psychiatrist called ketamine the most incredible advance in psychiatry in the last 50 years.

When did you go public with your depression, and why? You wrote about it in *The Hollywood Reporter*.[1]

That was the first time I went truly public. I wrote about my depression right after Robin Williams died by suicide, which was shortly after I finished ECT. I thought, "Robin Williams, if he did it, it could affect anybody."

But what I wrote, I shared only with friends. Then within a week of each other, Kate Spade and Anthony Bourdain died by suicide. I thought, "This is an epidemic that I have to speak out against. I have to destigmatize this. I have to share my experience."

And to your point, I'm a normal-looking "successful guy" who's got a family and has run businesses. So, if it can affect me, it can affect anybody. And I don't mean "affect anybody" in that you have to be depressed, but you know somebody who's depressed, or it's in your family, or you're living with somebody who's depressed.

I was talking about this with my doctor when he said, "Get ECT." He said, "You may have to skip work for a month." I said, "I can't. What am I going to tell them?" He said, "Well, let me ask you a question. If you had to get a stent put in your heart because you were having a heart attack, would you stop going to work and go to the hospital?" I said, "Of course." He said, "This is the same thing. This is a medical illness. It just happens to be in your brain as opposed to another part of your body."

The veil of shame is so intense. When you went public, you were working for yourself at that time. Do you think that made a difference?

I think it made it easier because I didn't have to check with HR and the PR department, and go to the CEO and say, "Hey, this may affect the stock price." It was my decision. But even if I had been working at a big company at that point, I would have pushed. Unless they just said, "You absolutely can't do it" for whatever reason, I would have said, "OK, now's the time to tell my story."

How does your life story inform the culture that you've created at your own company?

I'm very honest. My team knew I was going for treatments. I said, "I'm sorry, I can't come to this meeting. I'm going to be in treatment, and I may be a little loopy the rest of the afternoon, so I can't do it." I wasn't saying, "I have a doctor's appointment; I'll be busy." I was very open about it.

You begin to destigmatize it by talking about it as if it were normal, which it should be. It's like, "Oh, I can't be here today. I have my therapy appointment this afternoon." If you say it casually like that, people look at you funny for a second, but then they start to use it as the vernacular of normal conversation. People started to ask me about my treatment and felt like they were intruding. But I would say, "No, please, I want to talk about it. This is what it was like, and this is what happened." It's unbelievable how many people have come up to me and said, "Can you make a recommendation for a doctor for me?"

What about a young person who's not the boss, who can't stand up and say, "I'm going for my treatment," because they may feel that would hurt their future? What's your advice for them and the boss who wants to support that person in the right way? What would you say to people in management positions who want to help?

I would use the old cliché, "If you don't have your health, you don't have anything." Therefore, do everything you need to do to get the help you need. You don't have to tell everybody, because you don't want to overshare, but tell the people you need to tell. And honestly, if company leaders don't support you, get out, because it's not a culture in which you want to build a career or spend another minute of your life. Go somewhere else that will support you, because it's just too important.

I would tell managers to destigmatize it. Talk about it in normal terms. Be sensitive, and explain to your team, "Listen, we're all in this together. Please come to me with anything you need personally that will help you."

At the end of the day, it's a business. The manager wants everyone to be as productive as possible. Create an environment where somebody can say, "I'm not doing so well today." If you have a meeting and somebody—say, your head data scientist—is miserably depressed, she's not really going to contribute much to your meeting. So, give her the space to say, "I'm just feeling horrible today. I'm just not there for whatever reason" or "I need to do this treatment."

It's good to know, as a manager, which of your team members is and is not there on certain days, and who can contribute and who can't. But it's also the right thing to do as an empathetic human being.

———————

Morra Aarons-Mele is an entrepreneur, online marketing expert, and communications executive who founded the award-winning strategic communications agency Women Online and The Mission List, an influencer database. She helped Hillary Clinton log on for her first internet chat, and has launched digital campaigns for former President Obama, Malala Yousafzai, the United Nations, and many other leading figures and organizations. An extremely anxious introvert herself, Morra hosts the top-rated podcast *The Anxious Achiever* for HBR Presents from *Harvard Business Review*. She's passionate about helping people rethink the relationship between their mental health and their leadership.

Paul Greenberg is CEO of the digital video firm Butter Works and has dealt with mental health issues his entire life. He has tried many treatments for his severe depression, the most successful of which have been electroconvulsive therapy (ECT) and ketamine, and he is an advocate for destigmatizing these diseases and helping people get the treatment they need.

NOTE

1. Paul Greenberg, "A CEO's Radical Treatment for a Lifetime of Depression," *The Hollywood Reporter*, July 23, 2018, https://www.hollywoodreporter.com/lifestyle/lifestyle-news/paul-greenberg-details-lifelong-psychiatric-struggle-radical-treatment-1127797.

CHAPTER 19

Offering the Mental Health Benefits BIPOC Employees Need

by Andrea Holman and Joe Grasso

"I am not OK. But I know I have to be. And I will be. But I'm not OK."

One of us (Andrea) shared these conflicted yet honest sentiments with a colleague after the murder of Ahmaud Arbery began to receive increased media attention in April 2020. The feeling I called "not OK" was actually

Adapted from "Are You Offering the Mental Health Benefits Your BIPOC Employees Need?," on hbr.org, September 11, 2020 (product #H05UQZ).

psychological distress. I was nervous, mentally fatigued, and continually distracted by the pain of another racially motivated murder and the fear that this could happen to someone I loved. While I was not directly connected to Ahmaud Arbery, the tragedy felt personal due to a psychological phenomenon called shared racial fate.

Managing my distress was further complicated by the burden I felt at work of having to maintain exemplary performance, a burden made even heavier by the realization that my family's finances and my professional reputation hinged on my ability to compartmentalize and suppress my emotions while working.

Even with my background in mental health, I didn't accurately label what I was experiencing—race-based traumatic stress—until I spoke with a therapist.

Fortunately, my mental health care benefits allowed me to reach out to a professional who helped me process my reactions and develop strategies to manage my emotions and take care of myself.

Unfortunately, many Black Americans don't have access to these same types of resources. Nor are Black Americans the only ones who experience race-related stress. Millions of people from racial minority groups carry the psychological weight of racism throughout their lives, including at work, and very few are able to reach out to culturally responsive mental health providers through their employee benefits.

In recent years, many companies have pledged to better support their employees who are Black, Indigenous, and People of Color (BIPOC), particularly with mental health. To do this well, they must offer services that meet the unique mental health needs of those employees.

At Lyra Health, one of us (Joe) consults regularly with employer benefits teams that are increasingly recognizing the shortcomings of a one-size-fits-all mental health program. So what do more effective programs look like? We believe they need to do two key things: Offer culturally appropriate benefits and ensure that employees who need those benefits are using them.

Offer Mental Health Benefits That Work

Most large employers offer mental health benefits via an employee assistance program (EAP), but these programs are often ill-suited to BIPOC communities' specific needs. While rates of mental illness among Black Americans are comparable to other racial groups, this community faces higher prevalence of severe symptoms that result in disability. The data is particularly troubling when coupled with the fact that BIPOC individuals are often less likely to seek treatment than other groups because of stigma, understandable cultural mistrust of health-care providers, and a lack of access to culturally responsive care. Many of these barriers are rooted in a history of maltreatment by the mental health profession.

Studies show that even when BIPOC people do obtain services, they often prematurely discontinue care and are less likely to receive a full course of treatment as recommended by clinical guidelines. Traditional EAPs often exacerbate this issue by offering six or fewer sessions to address an identified problem. Thus, treatment coverage often ends well before many evidence-based treatment protocols can be completed.

To make sure that your company's mental health benefits address these barriers, look at the following dimensions of your benefits solution:

- **Access:** Is it quick and easy to find and schedule an appointment with a provider? Do you offer online booking and matching of employees to available providers who fit their care needs? A mental health benefits solution should be able to demonstrate a reasonable average wait time for an appointment, with the ability to obtain a next-day appointment for urgent or severe issues.

- **Cultural responsiveness:** Are providers in the network vetted for their use of culturally responsive approaches to care, such as an ability to assess cultural factors that impact clients' lives, experience and training related to race-based stress, and competence in adapting treatment to cultural needs? Further, what continuing education does the vendor offer to ensure that their providers have easy access to high-quality, culturally informed training? Trainings should address issues related to race and ethnicity, but also promote culturally sensitive care related to other aspects of identity, such as best practices for evaluating and treating transgender people.

- **Provider diversity:** Does your mental health solution recruit and engage racially diverse providers? Ask about their initiatives to promote diversity within their provider network and whether they continually assess the balance of racial representation among their providers.

- **Effectiveness:** Are providers assessed for use of evidence-based therapies that are shown to be effective for diverse populations? Does your benefits solution track clinical outcomes specific to your employee population? An EAP should have data to show that most employees' mental health symptoms reliably improve.

- **Flexibility:** Are employees able to engage in care on their terms? That can mean being able to receive care in person, by phone, or by video call.

- **Specialty coverage:** Can your employees easily find providers who are trained to treat specific issues, such as post-traumatic stress disorder, or specific populations, such as children and adolescents?

Enhance Utilization Through Education and Partnership

Offering the right mental health benefits is the first step, but even the best benefits won't be effective if they're not utilized. Many EAPs have incredibly low usage rates, including among employees who identify as BIPOC, which some experts believe is due to stigma as well as a lack of awareness; many employees simply don't know that the EAP is available to them. Employers need to promote their mental health benefits using both data and storytelling to normalize mental health and explain how evidence-based therapy can effectively treat a wide spectrum of mental health conditions, from mild anxiety to insomnia to trauma.

Employers should also consider partnering with their BIPOC employee resource groups or affinity groups. These groups can provide safe spaces for discussion around employees' race-based traumatic stress and the intersection of mental health and cultural diversity. Ask the leaders of these groups if they'd be willing to have an HR representative and possibly a clinician from your mental health benefit provider join a meeting to discuss barriers that are holding BIPOC employees back from seeking help and how to overcome them. If your program effectively covers the dimensions described earlier, you can use this meeting to highlight features such as the ability to be matched with a provider who is culturally responsive.

We also find that outreach efforts are much more effective if BIPOC leaders champion them. When a BIPOC executive shares a personal story about mental health, it can help to challenge stigma and encourage access to these benefits.

As companies seek to build and support a more diverse and inclusive workforce, leaders need to understand that race-based stress can be a unique, pervasive burden for many of the employees they want to champion. Offering and promoting mental health benefits that are evidence-based, culturally responsive, and supported by company leaders can lead to meaningful progress in prioritizing the minds, bodies, and souls of BIPOC employees.

———————

Andrea Holman began working for Lyra Health as a diversity, equity, inclusion, and belonging program manager for workforce transformation in June 2021. Previously, she served as a tenured associate professor of psychology at Huston-Tillotson University in Austin, Texas, where she taught undergraduates. Therapy has helped her manage symptoms of anxiety and stress for several years.

Joe Grasso is a clinical psychologist and the senior director for workforce transformation at Lyra Health, where he partners with employers in shaping workforce mental health strategy and deploying psychoeducational programs. Prior to joining Lyra, Grasso conducted health services research and managed the implementation of a national training program for mental health clinicians. He has benefited from therapy personally, particularly during challenging life transitions.

CHAPTER 20

Forming an Employee Resource Group for Mental Health

by Jen Porter, Bernie Wong, and Kelly Greenwood

Every month, members of the employee resource group (ERG) at Best Buy's corporate headquarters meet to share their stories. The group's discussions have ranged from the Black community and mental health, to veterans, to the relationship between mental health and sexual assault, to how members manage OCD, to how

Adapted from "How to Form a Mental Health Employee Resource Group," on hbr.org, May 19, 2020 (product #H05MT7).

mental health impacts women. Throughout the Covid-19 pandemic, the group met virtually to discuss their mental health during the crisis. Coming out of a meeting, one employee said, "This is the most impactful thing I have done here."

ERGs are created to build community among people with shared identities or experiences at work. When done thoughtfully, those that focus on mental health promote diversity and inclusion and provide support for employees managing symptoms of mental health conditions. The most effective are well poised to address the three top methods of reducing the stigma around mental health: social connection, education, and peer support.

Despite the significant need for more programs like these, they are not yet widespread in the United States. Consider that 76% of U.S. employees experienced symptoms of a mental health condition in 2021, and yet 8 in 10 workers did not seek treatment due to shame.[1] But generational differences are striking and show that change is underway: A 2021 study of U.S. employees found that 68% of Millennials and 81% of Gen Zers have left roles for mental health reasons, compared with 50% of respondents overall.[2]

At Mind Share Partners, we believe that mental health ERGs are an important part of the solution. We've spent the last few years working with leading companies as they launch and grow their programs. Today, more companies are realizing they need to do the same. Next, we'll share the critical steps we've seen businesses with effective mental health ERGs take, and how you can do the same.

Understand what mental health really means

Many companies view mental health ERGs as a subset of other communities, such as those involving employees who manage disabilities, participate in general wellness, or are neurodiverse. As a result, employers who have programs targeting such communities may think they are also supporting people managing mental health conditions when, in fact, they are not doing enough.

Unlike many disabilities, most mental health challenges are treatable, and the vast majority of people will experience one in their lifetime. Framing mental health as a disability can actually deter those whose experience of mental health is invisible or temporary, or those who see mental health as having positive attributes. In a similar vein, framing mental health as a part of wellness, and only focusing on upstream experiences like stress management, mindfulness, or resilience, can increase the stigma for those facing diagnosable conditions—especially if those are never named.

This is why we recommend creating an ERG with mental health as the primary focus or, at a minimum, defining mental health as a focus area of a more broadly defined ERG. Doing so helps narrow the focus and reduces barriers to entry for people who may not identify with the larger group. Further, according to Rachel Parrott, former diversity and inclusion manager at New Relic, ERGs that try to address all aspects of wellness or disability, without distinction, run the risk of "charter overload."

Build a coalition to get started

If your company has an established process for launching an ERG, be ready to make the case for why mental health is important. Find other employees to advocate with you in order to demonstrate that the need exists. When possible, getting an executive to sponsor the group is a good way to garner strong support.

If your company doesn't have established ERGs, start small with whatever avenues you have available. For example, begin a mental health Slack channel or hold an informal lunch-and-learn. Anything you can do to demonstrate interest and initiate conversation will go a long way in making a valid case.

As your group becomes formalized, make sure to get your legal and HR teams on board early in the process. If your legal or HR team is hesitant to engage with mental health, be prepared with examples of other companies that have mental health ERGs. (To get you started, see Mind Share Partners' list of mental health ERGs in the United States.[3]) Because mental health conditions are covered by the Americans with Disabilities Act, the legal department can ensure your name, mission, audience, and activities comply with privacy laws.

Specifically, employers must not create a situation where an employee might inadvertently or unwillingly disclose a mental health condition simply by joining an ERG or participating in a group activity. To avoid this, groups should be framed to serve people impacted by mental health, whether personally, as a caregiver, through a family member or friend, or as an ally. Zillow, for example, addresses this by including allyship in its group's name: Able and Disabled Advocates Partnering Together.

Make it safe for people to share their stories

Among the most powerful tools that an ERG has is the ability to create a forum for storytelling. In our work with companies, we've found that storytelling reduces isolation, creates community, and reduces the stigma of mental health issues. For employees who aren't seeking help because they feel ashamed, it tells them "You're not alone." For those who don't know where to get help, it gives them a path forward. For those who feel overwhelmed with the demands of being a caretaker, it builds connection.

There are several ways you can create a safe space for people to share their stories in your group. At some companies, such as Best Buy, the forum is private, with "Vegas rules," meaning information discussed during meetings is confidential. Alternatively, peer listening programs, such as the Peer Network at Reuters, facilitate private, peer-to-peer conversations about mental health.

Both types of forums set communication ground rules to guide employees on safe ways to engage with one another. Often, group members are asked to be mindful of giving advice and share mental health tips in general terms rather than acting like a therapist. Most importantly, they must follow company guidance for seeking help if someone is in danger of harm.

In other companies, employees choose to be more public. An employee at Lucidchart, for instance, led a lunch-and-learn during which she shared her experience with generalized anxiety disorder. As part of Pinterest's annual KnitCon event, two employees discussed mental health in the time of Covid-19 and shared a framework about how to reach out for help. And Yahoo! organizes meetings around a movie viewing or board game. The setup is meant to encourage group discussions around how the brain works or one aspect of mental health.

When considering how to facilitate storytelling in your own group, remember there is no right way to do it. Whatever you decide, get input from your members and test out ideas that work for everyone.

Educate everyone

Although mental health challenges are common, they are also associated with high levels of shame due to widespread misconceptions, such as that mental health conditions are rare or are only experienced by low performers. ERGs provide a way for you to educate your organization otherwise. By hosting lunch-and-learns, and sponsoring trainings and events, ERGs can reach people impacted by mental health challenges who might not be willing to join a group as a result of the stigma.

Organizations looking to ramp up their virtual resources can follow in the steps of companies like Retail-MeNot. Its mental health ERG, called RMN caRe, educates employees via a dedicated Slack channel, ongoing remote events with outside speakers, and written guidance on mental health benefits and policies.

We've also seen mental health ERGs partner with other identity-based groups to offer employees support.

This strategy is particularly effective because the prevalence and causes of mental health issues often differ among communities. For example, LGBTQ+ employees are three times more likely than others to experience a mental health condition. Women are more likely than men to have received a mental health diagnosis but are also more open to getting treatment. Mental health ERGs are especially well positioned to work with such groups and facilitate nuanced conversations about community-specific experiences.

Get companywide support

ERGs are just one component of a broader movement of culture change for mental health at work. While they are a powerful tool for education and community building, ERGs must receive both top-down and bottom-up support to be successful. It's imperative for executives, specifically, to verbalize the importance of mental health at their company and, where possible, share their own experiences to ensure that their message isn't viewed as simply "checking a box."

Those looking for inspiration can follow in the footsteps of Guru Gowrappan when he was CEO at Yahoo! He shared a video featuring employees discussing the need to reduce the stigma and invested in training for his executive team. Gowrappan wrote about the session in his weekly all-staff email, and several leaders followed suit by reaching out to their teams to communicate their support for mental health, expressing a desire to continue the conversation. "I could see how committed leaders were," one employee told us.

Still, just speaking out is not enough. Companies need to back up their claims with sufficient and easily accessible mental health benefits, so that employees who do need help can get it. While this may seem expensive, it won't go without reward. Companies that pursue organizationwide culture efforts can expect a 6:1 ROI.[4]

Like any initiative, ERGs that are underresourced and lack real influence will do little to change the overall culture at a company. However, if integrated with company priorities, and as part of a broader mental health strategy, they can be a powerful grassroots way of creating healthy workplaces for all.

Jen Porter is the COO and a principal at Mind Share Partners, a nonprofit that is changing the culture of workplace mental health so that both employees and organizations can thrive. It provides training and strategic advising to leading companies, hosts communities to support ERGs and professionals, and builds public awareness. Jen has helped to launch two mission-based organizations and, along the way, experienced depression during pregnancy as well as periods of burnout.

Bernie Wong is the senior manager of insights and a principal at Mind Share Partners. He maintains an intimate, long-standing relationship with chronic depression, inspiring both an education and a career focused on mental health through public health, sociology, and advocacy lenses.

Kelly Greenwood is the founder and CEO of Mind Share Partners. She has learned to manage her generalized anxiety disorder, which has twice led to debilitating depression. She founded Mind Share Partners to create the resources that she wished she, her managers, and her organization had had when she was struggling. Follow her on Twitter @KellyAGreenwood.

NOTES

1. Mind Share Partners, *Mental Health at Work 2021 Report*, https://www.mindsharepartners.org/mentalhealthatworkreport-2021; https://nami.org/Get-Involved/Pledge-to-Be-StigmaFree/Stigma Free-Company.

2. "StigmaFree Company," National Alliance on Mental Illness, https://www.nami.org/Get-Involved/Pledge-to-Be-StigmaFree/ StigmaFree-Company.

3. Bernie Wong, "An Evolving List of Employee Resource Groups for Mental Health in the U.S.," Mind Share Partners, March 4, 2019, https://www.mindsharepartners.org/post/list-of-mental-health -ergs-in-the-us.

4. "Mental Health and Employers: Refreshing the Case for Investment," Deloitte, January 2020, https://www2.deloitte.com/content/ dam/Deloitte/uk/Documents/consultancy/deloitte-uk-mental-health -and-employers.pdf.

CHAPTER 21

Rewriting the Company's Mental Health Policy

by Kelsey Raymond

Imagine how you'd react if one of your employees crawled into your office with a broken leg or became visibly ill at their desk. You wouldn't ignore their physical health or say they really need to keep their personal problems at home; you'd help the person to the emergency room and ask how you can support their recovery.

The truth is that your employees' health is rarely as obvious as a broken bone or the flu. Sometimes, your employees silently struggle with mental health conditions

Adapted from "How We Rewrote Our Company's Mental Health Policy," on hbr.org, July 11, 2016 (product #H02ZUJ).

that you never see, but their need for inclusive, supportive health care and adequate accommodations is just as great. Statistically, it's likely that at least one person on your team is living with a mental illness right now.

Without a proper mental health plan in place, your company is not only neglecting the well-being of its employees, but also missing out on the significant returns that fully healthy employees can deliver. As a leader in your organization, you have the authority and responsibility to improve your policy to better support employees. Here's how my company, Influence & Co., wrote an entirely new mental health policy and openly discussed it with our team—and how you can do the same.

Step 1: Define Your Goals

First, I partnered with our director of human resources to discuss the most important elements to include in this policy. Above all, we wanted to acknowledge that mental illness affects everyone differently, to use inclusive language, and to ensure all employees feel supported by the new plan.

To do that, invite employees to directly communicate with you their ideas for a mental health policy. Members of my team started sharing their ideas with me after we returned from our company retreat, where I talked about my family's history of mental illness during a team exercise to open the door for more discussions.

Including some of your employees in this process, whether through an activity at your next retreat or during a private meeting, can give you valuable insight into exactly how you can reach the goals you define.

Step 2: Research and Write

With goals and employee feedback in mind, your HR director should gain a frame of reference by researching the language and accommodations other companies' policies include. From there, they should dig into what mental health organizations recommend for supporting people living with mental illnesses.

This step is especially important if, like my company, you've never had a comprehensive mental health policy on record. Even if you do, regular research keeps you up to date on the latest from mental health experts and leading organizations to ensure that the policy's language and accommodations best support your employees.

After the research, your HR director should draft your policy. Remember, it's all a work in progress at this point. Limit your involvement to the review process and encourage them to incorporate your initial ideas in a way that promotes company values and works with other policies.

Step 3: Consult Your Attorney

Once we had our draft prepared, we sent it to our HR attorney, who provided additional expertise and recommendations to ensure that what the policy suggested and promised was legal and aligned with our existing policies. He helped us revise the language and include specific information about confidentiality. The last thing you want is to spend resources creating a policy you can't legally introduce or enforce. Get feedback from your legal counsel before moving on.

Step 4: Consult a Mental Health Advocate

Because we didn't have a mental health professional on staff, we knew we needed to consult an expert. This person played an integral role in helping our team refine and implement our policy. Her involvement was the most important component of this process.

To help us, the mental health advocate provided guidance on appropriate language, open communication techniques, accommodation options, and creative solutions for working alongside our employees to support them. A mental health advocate can illuminate details you may never have considered, which can mean the difference between a policy that's a nice gesture and a policy that's truly effective.

Step 5: Introduce Your Policy and Offer Training

Don't risk your employees misunderstanding specific policy benefits or accommodations by rolling out your new plan in an email. Create an event or host a workshop around it to clarify exactly what this policy means for each team member and how it came to be.

For this step, I recommend inviting your mental health advocate back for assistance; the training workshops our advocate created were essential parts of the process for our team, and we couldn't have done it without her.

My team decided to host two workshops: one exclusively for our senior leadership team and direct supports and one for all employees.

- **Train your leadership team first.** Before you introduce your plan to your whole company, make
sure managers and direct supports understand
their roles in implementing the policy. With your
mental health advocate and HR director, take your
leaders through each point of the plan and clearly
explain what is—and, just as important, is not—
expected of them. While they should feel prepared
to support coworkers and answer policy questions,
they shouldn't feel responsible for "fixing" any
employees' mental illnesses.

- **Train your employees.** Next, introduce the policy
to your entire team, and pair it with training on
mental health in the workplace. Our advocate gave
a presentation that covered recognizing signs of
mental illness in yourself, asking for help when
you need it, finding the right professionals, adapting your work life to accommodate illness, and
supporting others who are struggling. With this
new knowledge and a policy in place, our whole
team felt more prepared and supported.

Both sessions encouraged our team to talk openly
about mental health, and I received overwhelmingly
positive feedback from leadership and employees alike.
Members of our direct support team reached out to say
they felt much more empowered to help in mental health
situations. As one employee put it: "I just wanted to say
how much I appreciate the mental health policy. So few
people—much less employers—consider the importance
of mental health in the workplace. I love working for a
company that is so progressive and open in employee

health care. I feel more comfortable and valued as an employee."

Employee wellness is not a new concept. Companies around the country offer employees free gym memberships and yoga classes and incentives for healthy diets; what's sorely lacking is an equal focus on mental health programs. As a company leader, you have the power to change your organization's attitude and support system around mental health for the better—and at least one of your employees is waiting for you to realize it. The time is now.

Kelsey Raymond is the cofounder and CEO of Influence & Co., a full-service content marketing firm that specializes in helping companies strategize, create, publish, and distribute content that accomplishes their goals. Influence & Co.'s clients range from venture-backed startups to *Fortune* 500 brands.

Index

Index

Index

Notes

Smart advice and inspiration from a source you trust.